THE

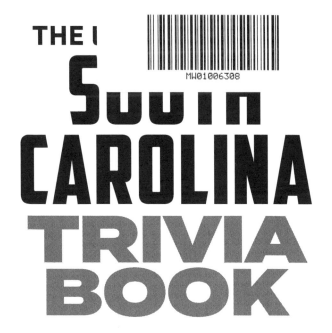

THE I
SOUTH
CAROLINA
TRIVIA
BOOK

Also Available in the College Trivia Series

THE UNIVERSITY OF
SOUTH
CAROLINA
TRIVIA
BOOK

ELIZABETH CASSIDY WEST

LYONS
PRESS

Essex, Connecticut

An imprint of Globe Pequot, the trade division of
The Rowman & Littlefield Publishing Group, Inc.
4501 Forbes Blvd., Ste. 200
Lanham, MD 20706
www.rowman.com

Distributed by NATIONAL BOOK NETWORK

British Library Cataloguing in Publication Information available

Library of Congress Cataloging-in-Publication Data

Names: West, Elizabeth Cassidy, author.
Title: The University of South Carolina trivia book / Elizabeth Cassidy
   West.
Other titles: College trivia.
Description: Essex, Connecticut : Lyons Press, [2024] | Series: College
   trivia series
Identifiers: LCCN 2023050200 (print) | LCCN 2023050201 (ebook) | ISBN
   9781493074495 (trade paperback ; alkaline paper) | ISBN 9781493074501
   (epub)
Subjects: LCSH: University of South Carolina—History—Miscellanea. |
   University of South Carolina—Miscellanea. | LCGFT: Trivia and
   miscellanea.
Classification: LCC LD5034 .W47 2024 (print) | LCC LD5034 (ebook) | DDC
   378.757/71—dc23/eng/20231108
LC record available at https://lccn.loc.gov/2023050200
LC ebook record available at https://lccn.loc.gov/2023050201

♾️™ The paper used in this publication meets the minimum requirements of
American National Standard for Information Sciences—Permanence of Paper
for Printed Library Materials, ANSI/NISO Z39.48-1992.

This book is an unofficial guide to University of South Carolina history and
trivia and is not endorsed by the school.

CONTENTS

PREFACE

History is messy, funny, strange, sad, and sometimes inspiring. The University of South Carolina has over two centuries of history and trivia to explore. The questions, answers, and quotes in this book are in no way definitive. In fact, I hope these snapshots of the university's life will prompt some chuckles and raised eyebrows and pique an interest in learning more about our great university. For those who don't yet have a connection with the university, this book will serve as a fun and informative introduction to its students, traditions, campus, faculty, leaders, and alumni. And, of course, athletics. *Here's a health, Carolina, forever to thee!*

INTRODUCTION

The birth of South Carolina College in 1801 went quite smoothly and quickly. It was the easiest moment in its history. After that, antebellum administrators had difficulty in managing privileged, hot-headed youth who chafed against its strict regulations. The campus was closed during the Civil War and barely escaped the fires that burned one-third of the city of Columbia in 1865. The second half of the nineteenth century was one long identity crisis as the institution struggled to survive the political forces bearing down upon it, from the highs of the Reconstruction era integration to the lows of desperately poor budgets at the turn of the century.

The University of South Carolina faced the twentieth century with its identity secured, moving and growing through the tumults of world wars, the Great Depression, the enrollment of women, and desegregation and civil rights to finally become a university for all the people of South Carolina.

Today, the university continues its founding mission of preparing future generations of leaders in South Carolina and beyond with its nationally recognized teaching, research, community engagement, and student life programs.

 STUDENT LIFE AND TRADITIONS

What common social activities were banned by the board of trustees in the 1800s?

Gambling, drinking, horseracing, and cockfighting were common social activities in the nineteenth century. The board of trustees banned all of them at South Carolina College, and as a result, student discipline was a constant problem.

What was the first student organization?

The Philomathic Society was established in 1805. It was split into the Clariosophic and Euphradian Literary Societies the following year.

What were literary societies?

They were essentially debating groups. Nearly every antebellum student joined one of them. Debates included hot political issues like slavery and national defense, as well as social topics such as divorce and the proper ways to court ladies.

What types of behavior were not allowed during society meetings?

The societies developed a system of levying fines for wide ranges of improper conduct in the meeting halls. Finable offenses included sitting in an indecent posture, laughing, spitting on the carpet, and hitting the person assigned to critique members' orations.

Why was the glass tax added to enrollment fees in 1825?

Students broke so many windows each year that a mandatory window breakage fee, or "glass tax," was levied in anticipation of replacing multiple shattered windowpanes.

Why were antebellum students required to eat at the on-campus dining facility?

To prevent students from being overcharged by the few boarding houses in the city; to keep students on campus so as not to disrupt the class schedules by being late returning from the city, and, most importantly, to keep them away from the city taverns.

How did students protest poor food?

By throwing their plates and silverware down the college wells, or by engaging in biscuit fights.

This college is in "yearly jeopardy of being destroyed because of disputes about eating."
—President Thomas Cooper, 1821

What student act became known as the Great Biscuit Rebellion?

Prior to the Civil War, students were required to eat at the only campus dining facility, which frequently served wormy biscuits and rancid meat. Students had complained for years, and petitioned the trustees to be allowed to eat off campus. Finally, in 1852, they staged what became known as the Great Biscuit Rebellion. Of the 199 students enrolled at the college, 109 students signed an honor-bound agreement that if the food system was not changed, they would all leave. The trustees refused to comply, so all 109 students left.

What was the cause of the only fatal duel between two Carolina students?

James G. Adams and A. Govan Roach were best friends who reached for a plate of fish at the same time. Serving rights belonged to whomever touched a plate first, but because neither student would relinquish his hold on the plate, they challenged each other to a duel. Adams was severely wounded and died within a few hours. Roach never recovered from his wounds and died a few years later.

What was the most popular prank at Carolina during the early 1800s?

Stealing turkeys from the homes of professors and citizens of Columbia. Occasionally, the students would return the birds alive but completely featherless.

> "Little good done this week. ! am weary of reporting the determined persevering idleness of these young men, and of dragging them to their duties."
> —Professor George Blackburn, 1814

What was a "tin pan serenade"?

Nineteenth-century students often "serenaded" unpopular professors by beating on tin pots and pans under their windows at midnight.

How did early South Carolina College students try to avoid going to class?

They removed the wooden steps to Rutledge College during the night, and they stole the college bell that was used to call them to class or chapel. The college eventually replaced the wooden steps with stone.

What cruel prank was known as "calf-tailing"?

South Carolina College students often tied a mothball to the tail of a calf or a dog, lit the ball on fire, and chased the terrified animal across the campus.

When were fraternities established at Carolina?

The first chapter was formed in 1850, but fraternities didn't become popular until the 1880s.

What students were known as Barbarians?
Non-fraternity students.

Why were fraternities banned in 1897?
When fraternities became popular enough in the 1880s to challenge the campus dominance of the literary societies, the societies' members petitioned the board of trustees to ban the Greeks. They accused the Greeks of acting socially superior, promoting drinking, damaging college spirit, and encouraging dishonest behavior. The fight eventually reached the state legislature, which passed a law in 1897 banning all Greek-letter fraternities from all state-supported colleges. The act included a specific exemption for literary societies.

What kind of organizations were I Tappa Kegga and the Sons of Schlitz?
They were sub rosa fraternities. During the ban on Greek-letter societies, many fraternities went underground and pretended to be campus clubs. Some chose unusual names like the ones above.

How long did the ban last?
Greek letter societies were banned from Carolina for thirty years. When the ban ended in 1927, various "clubs" petitioned to become chapters of national social and honor fraternities and sororities.

What was the Carolina-Clemson Football Riot of 1902?

When Carolina scored an upset 12-6 victory over Clemson, students paraded down Main Street with a banner depicting a crowing rooster over a beaten tiger. The Clemson Cadet Corps, armed with bayonets and swords, marched on the campus with the intent of seizing the banner. Several dozen Carolina students hastily armed themselves with clubs, rocks, and a few pistols and hunkered down behind the low brick wall and prepared to defend their alma mater. Faculty members and police intervened before any blood was shed. The Carolina-Clemson football game was suspended until 1909.

What two traditions came out of the 1902 Carolina-Clemson riot?

To diffuse the conflict, a compromise was reached: the drawing was burned between the two groups of students while they cheered each other—the first tiger burn. It was also after this incident that the Carolina teams became known as the Gamecocks. Carolina had not yet settled on a mascot before the 1902 game, but when the newspapers started calling the team the Gamecocks because of the drawing, the name stuck.

Why was there a drawing of a gamecock on the picture if we weren't the Gamecocks?

There are two likely reasons for having the picture of the gamecock in the drawing. First was the prominence of Revolutionary War hero general Thomas Sumter who was known as the "Gamecock." Second was the fact that cockfighting was still widespread in the state.

What future Carolina president participated in the 1902 riot?

Sophomore J. Rion McKissick armed himself with a pistol to defend the campus from the invading Clemson students. He later served as president from 1936 to 1944.

Who was the first named mascot?

A variety of live gamecocks and homemade gamecock costumes made appearances at football games over the years, but Big Spur was the first named mascot. The eight-foot-tall bird first appeared in 1978.

Cocky and Big Spur at a basketball game, 1980. Courtesy of the University of South Carolina Archives.

When did Cocky debut?

Cocky first appeared alongside Big Spur at the 1980 Homecoming game. He did not make a good impression with fans who were used to the tougher-looking Big Spur. By the 1981 football season, however, he had won over the fans with his antics and interactions with the crowd.

How many times has Cocky been National Mascot of the Year?

As of this printing, four times, in 1986, 1994, 2003, and 2008.

What group of female students caused a scandal in 1929?

The University Coed Follies were a dance and tap group of female students. Most of the public response to the group was positive, but President Davison M. Douglas received complaints regarding their short costumes. The group agreed to drop the "University" from their name, and the Coed Follies performed throughout the state into the early 1930s.

What was the "defense haircut"?

During World War II, the need for metal in the defense industries created a shortage of hairpins, so female students wore their hair in the "defense haircut," a looser style that did not require the use of hairpins.

How else were students affected by World War II?

Students and faculty had to participate in the rationing that took place to conserve food and supplies during the war. Students formed a Red Cross chapter and held scrap metal drives, which collected used metal objects, such as razor blades, for recycling.

Who was carried onto the football field in a giant football in 1948?

The identity of the 1948 Homecoming Queen was kept a secret until halftime, when a giant football was carried onto the field. It opened to reveal Homecoming Queen Jackie Johnson.

Who were known as the "rats" on campus?

Freshmen.

What were "rat caps?"

Rat cap was a nickname for the beanies that all male and female freshmen at Carolina were required to wear from the late 1890s until the 1960s. Freshmen were also frequently hazed by seniors.

"WRITE HOME AND LET MOTHER KNOW YOU ARE ALL RIGHT."
—1921–22 student handbook

What was Barefoot Day?

Freshmen were required to wear their beanies every day until a day in April called "Barefoot Day." On that day, they were allowed to remove their rat caps but were required to walk around barefoot and take orders from seniors. The tradition was rocked by scandal in 1936 when some seniors ordered a group of freshmen to hug and kiss all the female students they saw. Some women were accidentally knocked down, and others fled to the library where the librarian locked the door to keep the men outside. Parents and the public were outraged; some parents pulled their daughters out of the university. President McKissick conducted an investigation, and several students were suspended.

What was the Miss Venus Pageant?

The Miss Venus Pageant was a legs beauty contest held from the 1940s to the early 1970s as part of the Greek-sponsored Derby Day festivities. Female contestants wore tight blouses, short shorts, and high heels, and paraded in front of the judges with paper bags over their heads so that they could be judged for their "other attributes."

Who were the judges for the Miss Venus Pageant?

The contestants were judged by Sigma Chi brothers and university administrators, including the president and the dean of women.

Name the three students who desegregated the university in 1963.

Robert Anderson, Henri Monteith, and James Solomon were the first African American students to enroll since Reconstruction.

Anderson, Monteith, and Solomon exit the administration building during the 1963 desegregation of the university. Courtesy of the University of South Carolina Archives.

Name the first African American student body president.

Harry Walker, in 1971.

When was the largest riot in school history?

On May 7, 1970, a group of students locked the doors and occupied the Russell House student union building for about five hours, following a campus protest over the shooting of students at Kent State University by National Guardsmen. Several days later, on May 11, hundreds of students staged the largest riot in school history, taking over and trashing part of the Osborne Administration Building, and trapping the president and some trustees in their offices. National Guardsmen used tear gas to clear students from the Horseshoe area of campus and restore order.

What popular freshman course was born from the 1970 riot?

While President Thomas Jones was trapped in his office during the riot, he decided that the university should have a program to help students adjust to university life. That idea eventually became University 101.

Who was the first African American Homecoming Queen?

Gail Ransome, in 1973.

What national record did Carolina students set in 1974?

On March 4, 1974, 505 Carolina students set the record for the largest group streak on a college campus. The group streaked from the Roost and Bates House, up the mezzanine stairs in Thomas Cooper Library, past the Russell House, through Columbia Hall, and across the Horseshoe. CBS News did a story on the event, prompting first lady Mary Jones to comment that the news coverage was in good taste, but the bodies were not. The Gamecocks' record was soon beaten by the University of Georgia, when 1,500 naked students ran across their campus, a record that still stands.

When were students allowed to buy beer on campus?

In 1973, the university opened the Golden Spur student lounge in the Russell House as an alternative to the "unhealthy and unwholesome" Columbia bars. It quickly became a popular spot for students and faculty, but closed in the mid-1980s when the minimum drinking age was raised to twenty-one.

Where was the student canteen and lounge in the 1930s and 1940s?

The popular student hangout was in the basement of Maxcy College, one of the buildings constructed through the New Deal building program in the late 1930s.

Who was the first Homecoming Queen?

Mary King became the University of South Carolina's first Homecoming Queen in 1941. The second queen was not elected until 1945, because the Homecoming activities were suspended during World War II.

Who were the Corsairs and the Corsettes?

During World War II, the Naval ROTC program formed a drill platoon named the Corsairs. A mock female drill team named the Corsettes was formed shortly after.

Did the University of South Carolina ever have a dress code?

Yes, students were expected to dress neatly for class. Men had to wear suits or slacks and ties, and women had to wear dresses. The dress code did not survive the 1970s, as the administration listened to student demands for relaxed regulations.

When were telephones put in dormitories?

Hall telephones were used from the 1930s to the 1950s.

When did parking become a problem on campus?

As soon as the first car showed up, there have been complaints about parking. However, it became a major issue for students and employees during the rapid growth of the student body and the dramatic expansion of the campus in the 1960s and 1970s.

What scandalous student prank burst onto the campus scene in the 1950s?

Panty raids. Groups of male students would try to get inside women's dormitories to steal their lingerie.

When was the first panty raid at the University of South Carolina?

May 19, 1952. Approximately 350 male students stormed the Wade Hampton and Sims women's dormitories in a quest for "unmentionables." University and Columbia police were called in to prevent them from taking over the dorms, although a few men did get inside women's rooms and successfully got away with some underwear. A group climbed through a window into one student's room and emptied her entire lingerie drawer out of the very same window. Someone pulled a fire alarm, bringing three fire trucks to women's quad, and one female student reportedly dumped a bucket of water out of her window, drenching a police officer.

How did the university respond?

After a one-day investigation, the discipline committee suspended six male students, for time periods varying between three and six months.

Did that end the panty raids?

Not in the least. Around five hundred students signed a petition protesting the suspensions, saying the prank was not malicious, but a demonstration of school spirit. The suspensions were not overturned. More raids continued, including one in 1955 of nearly one thousand men on Sims dormitory, but they failed to enter the building. Women students taunted them, lured them close to the windows by tossing down underwear, and then poured water on their heads. The popularity of the raids finally died out in the early 1960s.

Who said, "the human knee is never an attractive sight?"

Dean of Women Arney Childs. She was commenting on the university's dress code that banned short pants and skirts above the knee, in the 1950s.

What was FREAK?

The Freedom to Research Every Aspect of Knowledge was a pro-drug use organization in the 1960s and 1970s. In 1970, they marched on the President's House and briefly took over the Russell House after the arrests of a student and two former students.

What is the Carolinian Creed?

The Carolinian Creed was developed in 1990 as an aspirational values statement to remind students of the importance of civil discourse while embracing mutual respect for everyone, even those they disagree with.

As a Carolinian . . .

I will practice personal and academic integrity;

I will respect the dignity of all persons;

I will respect the rights and property of others;

I will discourage bigotry, while striving to learn from differences in people, ideas and opinions;

I will demonstrate concern for others, their feelings, and their need for the conditions which support their work and development.

When was *The Gamecock* established?

The first issue of *The Gamecock* student newspaper was published on January 30, 1908. The newspaper was established by the Clariosophic and Euphradian literary societies, who also published a literary magazine called *The Carolinian*. *The Gamecock* eventually became independent when the societies' influence on campus declined.

What student tradition did World War II veterans refuse to participate in?

After serving in the military and war zones, veterans did not submit to traditional freshman hazing and beanies.

When was WUSC radio founded?

Student radio station WUSC was founded in 1947. It was first housed in the old slave quarters behind the President's House.

What were the Easter and May Queens?

The Easter Queen was elected during Easter Week festivities, a spring celebration. It eventually became May Day celebrations with a May Queen. The May Day festivals were large and elaborate. Students wove colorful ribbons around the Maypole, and the May Queen and her court wore elegant dresses. May Day was last held in 1969.

What student group toured across Europe in the 1920s?

The Gamecock Orchestra was founded in 1924 by a group of students. The orchestra played at student dances on into the 1930s, and it toured the United States and Europe in the late 1920s. After a performance at the French Riviera, a reporter wrote that the "rattling good jazz outfit . . . played as lively music as could be heard anywhere."

Where did campus dances take place?

Dances were a prominent part of campus social life, even during the Great Depression when students had to dress up in homemade dresses and borrowed tuxedos. A few dances were held in the elegant Jefferson Hotel ballroom, but most took place at the campus gymnasium (now Longstreet Theatre). They were sponsored by fraternities and other student clubs. After dancing together, students signed each other's dance cards.

What other social activities were popular before World War II?

Few students had cars, so many activities had to take place within walking distance of campus. Students enjoyed the movie theaters on Main Street, shared a Coca-Cola or a milkshake at Burnett's drug store, or went bowling. On campus, students played piano in the women's dorm lounge, had picnics, or sat on the Horseshoe benches, talking and holding hands.

Where are some current student hangouts?

The Five Points and Vista shopping and dining districts that border the university campus have long been popular places for students to gather. Students, faculty, and staff also frequent the Soda City Market on Main Street. Established in 2005, the weekly Saturday market for local farmers and crafters coined its name from the city's nickname. Columbia's postal abbreviation of "Cola" gave rise to the nickname "Soda City."

What is Thursday After Dark?

TAD is a late-night entertainment program held every Thursday that offers a wide variety of activities for students, including escape rooms, trivia, and baseball games.

How were women's residence halls stricter than the men's?

All dormitories had stricter regulations in the 1930s and 1940s, but female students were subjected to more stringent rules than their male counterparts. Every girl who went out after dark had to sign out with her name and her planned destination, and sign back in. The women students were not allowed to leave their dorms between 11:00 p.m. and 7:00 a.m.

What did the 1940 YMCA student handbook say was the school motto?

"Make all checks payable to the University of South Carolina."

What is the first record of a student disciplinary action?

William Davis was reprimanded in 1806 for "exhibiting marked disrespect" during chapel.

What caused the Riot of 1814?

Mathematics professor George Blackburn had an irascible temper and little patience with student shenanigans. He was the faculty member who pressed most of the disciplinary charges against misbehaving students. After getting three students suspended in 1814 for stealing the college bell, open rebellion broke out on the campus. Students gathered at the college well to consume alcohol, burnt an effigy of Blackburn, and destroyed the college bell. Students then beat the outside of Blackburn's home with brickbats, endangering his family. The militia had to be called in to take charge of the situation. Several students were suspended and expelled.

When were the college cadets formed?

Students formed a cadet corps in 1825 in preparation for the visit from Revolutionary War hero the Marquis de Lafayette on his grand tour through America. They practiced their drills and paraded for Lafayette's review.

What was the Guard House Riot of 1856?

Several South Carolina College students held a grudge against one of the Columbia city marshals. Violence between the students and the marshal escalated into a standoff between several hundred students and citizens, with both sides carrying weapons. The students had broken into the cadet corps armory before marching to the guard house with rifles. President Charles McCay was being ignored, but someone brought in former president James Thornwell from the seminary, and he was able to disperse and calm the students and lead them back to the campus.

Why was the college cadet corps disbanded?

After the guard house riot, Governor Adams seized the guns from the cadet corps and the corps was disbanded. Several students were expelled or suspended after the riot.

"May *The Gamecock* survive longer than any chicken that I have been able to keep on campus."
—Professor Edward S. Joynes, 1908

When was the cadet corps reestablished?
Just a few years after the guardhouse riot, the trustees authorized the students to form a new cadet company in 1860.

What were the Hypatian and Euphrosynean Societies?
Women students formed their own literary societies in 1916 and 1924. After women were allowed to enroll at Carolina, the Clariosophics and Euphradians banned women from their societies.

What was the German Club?
A dance club established in 1884, the German Club was named after a popular dance, not the language. Other dance organizations—the Damas Club, the Greeks, and the campus social cabinet—also held formals. The clubs' dances were limited to members, but the social cabinet's dances were open to all students.

Who was the first editor of *The Gamecock*?
Robert E. Gonzales.

What was the first women students' social event?
It was a dance at a local Columbia home in 1896.

What was the Parmethian Society?
It was the first female student organization, created in 1900. However, there were not enough women students enrolled at the time to keep it functioning, and it soon disbanded.

When was the *Garnet and Black* yearbook established?

It ran from 1899 to 1994. It was independent from the literary societies, unlike *The Carolinian* and *The Gamecock*.

Why was hazing a major problem in the early 1900s?

It could be violent, and in some cases, freshmen at Carolina were beaten bloody with electric wires. Students who reported violations were subjected to retaliation. It became a major problem on college campuses in the South in the early 1900s and was banned in South Carolina in 1914 by the state legislature.

What was the Carolina Bloomer Society?

It was a nickname for the women's gym classes based on their exercise clothes in the 1920s.

Who was Dixie Dugan?

She was the first switchboard operator at the university. When the switchboard was installed in 1929, Dugan not only operated the telephone system but became a hub of official and unofficial campus information and a beloved source of advice and comfort for homesick freshmen for many years.

What is known as the mighty sound of the Southeast?

The Carolina marching band.

Who was the first female student body president?

Rita McKinney, 1973.

What is the Carolina Clemson Blood Battle?

Since 1984, the two universities have held a competitive blood drive during the week before their football game. The competition is one of the largest blood drives in the country and has collected more than one hundred thousand pints of blood. The Carolina–Clemson Blood Drive Committee is the second-largest student-run organization at USC.

What is the largest student-run organization at Carolina?

The USC Dance Marathon, which was founded in 1999, has raised more than $7 million to support the pediatric patients of Prisma Health Children's Hospital in Columbia. The organization's annual spring dance marathon caps off its yearlong fundraising efforts.

FACULTY

Name the professor who once tried to have a student expelled for stupidity.

Francis Lieber was an internationally known scholar and professor of history and political economy, which he taught at South Carolina College from 1835 to 1855. However, he was tough, hot-tempered, and impulsive, and he once tried to have a student expelled for stupidity.

What nickname did students give Francis Lieber?

Old Bruin (Old Bear).

Which professor had to have an additional building constructed behind his Horseshoe residence to house his family?

Maximilian LaBorde needed the addition to house his ten children.

Which former faculty member's writings formed the foundation of laws on the conduct of war?

The Lieber Codes, written by Francis Lieber in 1862 and 1863 after he had left South Carolina College, set out the rules of conduct for US soldiers during the Civil War and today remains the basis of most regulations regarding the laws of war.

Which faculty member was nicknamed "Old Fossil"?

Chemistry professor Charles Brumby received the nickname in 1850 after a dispute with the junior class. Brumby tried to make the juniors attend extra lectures to make up for his absence due to illness. The students refused, boycotted his classes altogether, and burned their chemistry books in a bonfire. A song written about the uprising by student James Chalmers dubbed Brumby "Old Fossil."

Which professor described the faculty meetings as a "conclave of mummies"?

Francis Lieber.

Francis Lieber. Courtesy of the University of South Carolina Archives.

Which professor was known for cancelling classes on beautiful days?

English professor Havilah Babcock often cancelled his classes to go hunting or fishing. The avid outdoorsman even wrote a popular book, *My Health is Better in November: Thirty-Five Stories of Hunting and Fishing in the South*, first published in 1947. Babcock was a marvelous storyteller who warned his classes at the beginning of the semester, "My digressions are going to be a lot more interesting than anything else." He taught at the university from 1927 until his retirement in 1964.

Who headed the college during the Civil War?

As chairman of the faculty, Maximilian LaBorde headed the college during the Civil War, while it was without a president. LaBorde had to work with Confederate and, later, Union authorities regarding the use of the college buildings as a hospital. He joined the faculty in 1843 after serving as a state legislator, college trustee, and the secretary of state of South Carolina.

Who was Carolina's first African American faculty member?

Richard T. Greener, who taught mental and moral philosophy. He was the first African American graduate of Harvard University and one of the first African Americans to graduate from Carolina's law school. He also served as the college librarian for nine months. When Reconstruction ended and the university closed in 1877, Greener became dean of law at Howard University and later entered the US diplomatic corps, serving as the first US consul to Vladivostok, Russia, from 1898 to 1905.

Which faculty member died during a storm on the Horseshoe?

Botany professor Andrew Charles Moore joined the university in 1900 and established the university Herbarium with his own collections in 1907. The botanist had great affection for the university's campus and gardens. Moore died in his home in Lieber College, on the evening of September 17, 1928. That same evening, a terrible storm blew down his favorite tree on the Horseshoe; it fell on Lieber College.

Who was the author of the alma mater?

English professor George A. Wauchope is perhaps best known for writing the university's alma mater, "We Hail Thee Carolina," set to the tune of Robert Burns's "Flow Gently, Sweet Afton." The administration sponsored a contest in 1911, and Wauchope submitted the winning entry.

Which professor headed the South Carolina Red Cross in World War I?

Philosophy professor Josiah Morse. He arrived at Carolina in 1911 and served as the only faculty member of the Department of Philosophy for several years. Morse expanded the department during his thirty-five years of service to the university, adding courses on the psychology of religion and race problems in the South.

Dean of Women Irene Dillard Elliott, circa 1925.
Courtesy of the University of South Carolina Archives.

Who was the first woman dean?

English professor Irene Dillard Elliott was one of the first women to receive a PhD from the University of North Carolina. She joined the university faculty in 1924 and was appointed as Carolina's first dean of women. Elliott taught English at Carolina until her retirement in 1964.

Who was the first woman department head?

Katherine B. Heyward was one of the first female faculty members at the university and the first female department head in 1925. The university established its Department of Fine Arts in 1925 under Heyward. She retired in 1945 after twenty years on faculty.

Which professor was known as the "Incarnation of the Old South"?

Yates Snowden was one of the most recognizable figures on campus with his snow-white hair and black cape. He disapproved of the growing trend in higher education of requiring professors to have PhDs. Snowden spearheaded efforts to create a manuscripts repository at the college library.

Which faculty member was appointed US ambassador to South Korea?

In 1981, President Ronald Reagan named Richard "Dixie" Walker US ambassador to South Korea; he served in that role until 1986 when he returned to the university. President Donald Russell had recruited Walker away from Yale in 1957 to establish an international studies program. Walker founded the Institute of International Studies in 1961 and served as its director until 1981. The institute became a preeminent national and international center of research, conferences, consultation, and publications; it was named in his honor in 1996.

What was Francis Lieber's most hated part of his job at South Carolina College?

Faculty were required to make sure that students were in their dormitories at night and to try to catch them sneaking back on campus. Late one evening, Lieber heard a student who was carrying a stolen turkey trying to return to his room. When he chased the student, trying to apprehend him, he tripped and fell and exclaimed, "All this for two thousand dollars!"

Who was the second dean of women?

Arney R. Childs was hired by the university in 1935 in the dual role of history professor and dean of women. She was an inspiring teacher and counselor, accomplished author, a leader in several civic organizations, and the first treasurer of the South Carolina Historical Association as well as the first editor of its proceedings.

> **"It is my firm conviction that enforced segregation of the races in our public schools can no longer be justified on any basis—and should, therefore, be abolished as soon as practicable."**
> —Chester Travelstead, dean of education, 1956

Which dean was fired due to his pro-desegregation views?

Dean of Education Chester Travelstead became embroiled in a dispute over desegregation and free speech at the university. Travelstead believed that the state's efforts to fight desegregation were stifling the ability of faculty members to discuss racial segregation openly and critically. Governor George Bell Timmerman attempted to have the dean fired in May 1955 after receiving a letter from Travelstead that challenged the governor's position on desegregation. President Russell refused to fire him, but more controversy flared later that year when Travelstead gave a public lecture to some summer school students in which he attacked racial segregation at length. The board of trustees fired Travelstead, two weeks after his speech, stating that it was not in the university's best interest to employ him.

Which dean led the establishment of the MIBS program?

Business dean James Kane led the efforts in 1974 to establish an innovative program: the Master of International Business (MIBS). The new degree was a joint program with the Institute of International Studies that prepared students to compete in the global business arena. First offered in 1974, MIBS quickly became and remains a top-rated program in the United States.

"You have transformed quiet diplomacy into a fine art."
—Ronald Reagan to Richard L. Walker, 1983

Which professor brought Carolina's choral program worldwide acclaim?

When Hungarian native Arpad Darazs joined the USC faculty in 1966 as professor of music and director of choral activities, his guidance quickly elevated Carolina's choral program to the world stage. Students named him an outstanding teacher three times. Darazs also founded the Palmetto Mastersingers and served as the music director of the Columbia Philharmonic Orchestra. He taught at Carolina until his death in 1986.

Which law dean bragged about never having read the South Carolina code of laws?

Joseph Daniel Pope, law professor from 1884 until his death in 1908. He refused to adjust his teaching methods and only taught on equity and property. His students only attended class one hour a day. In 1901, an adjunct professor of law, M. Herndon Moore, joined the faculty and added code of laws to the curriculum.

Who was the first African American woman professor in arts and sciences?

Grace Jordan McFadden was the first African American woman professor in the College of Arts and Sciences and a former director of the African American Studies Program. McFadden organized a symposium in 1988 that marked the twenty-fifth anniversary of the desegregation of USC and directed the Oral History and Culture Project, which focused on the experiences of African Americans in the Southeast.

What famous author taught at the university in the 1960s?

James Dickey was poet and writer-in-residence in the 1960s. He wrote *Deliverance* while at the university.

Who was the first faculty member to teach a course on African American history?

Thomas Terrill taught The Negro in American History in 1968, the first African American–oriented course in university history.

Which professor produced some of the first daguerreotype images in the United States?

Chemistry professor William Ellet, in the 1840s. A daguerreotype was the first commercially successful photographic process. Each one is a unique image on a silvered copper plate and normally kept in a case.

Who is the ninety-year-old faculty member searching for the dark matter of the universe?

Physicist Frank Avignone, who has taught at Carolina since 1965. His experiments and research seek out the theoretical substance that is believed to make up the majority of the universe. Avignone is also the longest-serving faculty member.

Which professor was known for his one-man shows of historic figures?

Historian Edward Beardsley performed as Franklin Delano Roosevelt, Teddy Roosevelt, Woodrow Wilson, and Benjamin Franklin. His shows brought the historical figures to life at Carolina and in twenty-five other states. The popular professor and civil rights activist taught at the university from 1966 to 1998.

ALUMNI

Who was the first graduate of South Carolina College?

Anderson Crenshaw was the sole graduate in 1806, but he waited until the following year to participate in commencement.

Who was the first African American graduate?

T. McCants Stewart graduated with a bachelor of arts and a bachelor of law in 1874, when the university was briefly desegregated during Reconstruction. Stewart became an associate justice on the Supreme Court of Liberia.

Which Carolina alumnus was portrayed by Samuel L. Jackson?

Richard T. Greener in the 1994 movie *Assault at West Point: The Court-Martial of Johnson Whittaker*. The movie is based on the 1880 case of Black West Point cadet Johnson Whittaker, who was found beaten and tied to his bed. The academy didn't look for his attackers, instead accusing him of faking his own attack. Greener served as Whittaker's lawyer. Whittaker had also attended the Reconstruction-era university. Seth Gilliam portrayed Whittaker.

Which alumnus was portrayed by Billy Dee Williams?

Francis L. Cardozo, in the miniseries *North and South: Heaven and Hell*, which aired in 1994.

Who was the first woman to enroll?

Frances Guignard Gibbes was the first woman to enroll at Carolina in September of 1895. Gibbes, a Phi Beta Kappa, became a successful playwright and poet, earning national and international recognition for her work. Her play *The Face* was developed into a motion picture.

Who was the first woman to graduate?

In June 1898, Mattie Jean Adams became the first woman graduate of the university with a bachelor of arts. She then attended Oxford University, earned her master of arts degree from Columbia University, and received an honorary doctor of literature degree from Meridian College, where she was the head of the Department of English for eighteen years.

Name two alumni who appeared as themselves in episodes of *The Simpsons*.

Jasper Johns, who attended the university in 1947 and 1948, is an American painter, printmaker, and sculptor whose awards include the Presidential Medal of Freedom in 2011.

Leeza Gibbons, who graduated from the School of Journalism in 1982, is a nationally known television host with three Daytime Emmy Awards.

Women students on campus circa 1898. Mattie Jean Adams is on the far left. Courtesy of the University of South Carolina Archives.

Why was Preston S. Brooks expelled from South Carolina College in 1839?

Preston Brooks was a frequent disturber of the peace at the college in the late 1830s, though he always managed to avoid expulsion. That changed in 1839, when Brooks was about to graduate. After hearing an exaggerated report that his brother was being mistreated at the Columbia jail, Brooks stormed the jail with a pair of pistols. The police disarmed him, and the trustees finally expelled him.

What other violent act did he become infamous for?

Brooks was elected to the US Congress. In 1856, Massachusetts senator Charles Sumner delivered a speech against slavery in which he insulted Brooks's cousin, Senator A. P. Butler. Congressman Brooks responded by severely beating Senator Sumner with a cane on the floor of the US Senate. He received only a token punishment, resigned his seat, and was promptly reelected without opposition one month later.

Which faculty member is also one of the first African Americans to earn a law degree at the university?

Richard T. Greener, who earned his law degree in 1876.

Who is considered the father of USC Homecoming?

In the 1920s, Alumni Association secretary Bernard A. Early noted the rising popularity of football-weekend Homecoming at other schools. He accurately predicted a strong response from Carolina's alumni for this type of event. The Alumni Association had previously arranged various types of alumni reunions, but they didn't have activities like those of today's Homecoming celebrations. October 15, 1927, marked the first time a Carolina Homecoming was held in connection with a football game.

What are some former Homecoming traditions?

The Tea Dance was established as a Carolina Homecoming tradition in 1962. The Alumni Association took over planning for the dance that year and booked Buster Spann and the Original Gamecock Orchestra to provide the music. The Spann Orchestra was a reunion of former students who had belonged to Carolina's Gamecock Orchestra in 1930. The 1962 reunion proved so popular that the group continued to play at every Homecoming until 1988. Also that year, Carolina Capers, a student variety show, replaced the traditional pep rally. The Capers were replaced by Cockfest in 1971.

How many alumni served in World Wars I and II?

More than five hundred in World War I and more than six thousand in World War II.

Which alumnus is credited with saying, "South Carolina is too small to be a republic and too large to be an insane asylum"?

James L. Petigru, Class of 1809, who strongly opposed secession.

Who was the first alumnus to become governor of South Carolina?

Richard I. Manning, Class of 1811.

Who was the first alumnus to become president?

William C. Preston, Class of 1812, served from 1845 to 1851.

When was the last time an alumnus was president?

William H. Patterson was president from 1974 to 1977.

Which alumnus wrote the first history of the university?

Maximilian LaBorde, Class of 1821, published *A History of South Carolina College* in 1859.

How many antebellum alumni became South Carolina governors?

Twelve of the twenty-two governors between 1824 and 1865 (two-year terms).

Who was the first person to enroll at SCC?
William Harper, class of 1808.

Who was the first African American to enroll at USC?
Henry E. Hayne, secretary of state, enrolled in the medical school in 1873.

Who were some of the notable alumni of the Reconstruction-era university?
Joseph M. Morris, president of Allen University; Thomas E. Miller, president of State Agricultural and Mechanical College (now South Carolina State University); Cornelius Chapman Scott, minister; and William D. Crum, physician appointed by US president Theodore Roosevelt as collector of the Port of Charleston.

Who was the first woman to earn a law degree?
Minna Layton Holman, in 1918.

Who were the first graduates to earn a PhD?
Mason Crum (education) and Gilbert D. Voight (English), in 1925.

Who was the first woman to earn a PhD?
Dera Dry Parkinson, in 1927 (education).

Who was the only person to receive a PhB?

Charles Babbitt was the only person ever awarded a bachelor of philosophy, in 1875.

Who was the first woman to earn a master's degree?

Jacqueline Segar Epes, in 1903.

Who was the first woman to graduate with honors?

Anne Fayssoux Davis, in 1899.

Why was Frederick Hart pressured to drop out of Carolina in 1961?

Hart was the only white student arrested at a student civil rights demonstration held on March 3, 1961. After his arrest was reported in the newspapers, he received harassing calls, death threats from the Ku Klux Klan, and pressure from the dean of students to leave Carolina. He withdrew, moved to Washington, DC, and later became a well-known American sculptor. His work includes the famous *Three Soldiers* statue at the Vietnam Veterans Memorial.

Which future governor of South Carolina was expelled from the university for plagiarism?

Coleman L. Blease was expelled for plagiarism in 1888. He bore a vicious grudge against the school and, as governor, retaliated by vetoing numerous budget requests from the university and by accusing Carolina of diverting Peabody Fund monies away from Winthrop College. In reality, it was the other way around.

Name the alumni who are subjects of statues on the campus.

George Rogers. The statue of 1980 Heisman Trophy winner George Rogers depicts him standing on a bench in his number 38 jersey. The sculpture by W. Stanley "Sandy" Proctor was unveiled in 2015 at the Springs Brooks Plaza at Williams–Brice Stadium.

Richard T. Greener. The statue of Carolina's first African American professor, first African American librarian, and 1876 law graduate stands to the east of Thomas Cooper Library. Sculpted by Jon Hair, it is positioned so that Greener is gazing toward the Horseshoe, where he lived and taught from 1873 to 1877.

A'ja Wilson. Titled "Shoot for the Stars," the sculpture by Julie Rotblatt-Amrany honors Wilson's numerous academic and athletic accomplishments, including leading the women's basketball team to the 2017 NCAA National Championship, 2015 NCAA Final Four, three SEC regular-season championships, and four SEC Tournament titles. It was unveiled in front of the Colonial Life Arena in 2021.

Henri Monteith, Robert Anderson, and James Solomon. "The Remarkable Three" sculpture honors the first three African American students to enroll at USC since Reconstruction. It depicts the students stepping across the threshold of the university on September 11, 1963. The 2024 sculpture by Basil Watson is to the left of McKissick's main entrance and facing the Horseshoe.

Which alumnus was a defender of the Alamo?

James Butler Bonham attended South Carolina College from 1824 to 1827. He was expelled his senior year after leading a student protest over strict attendance regulations and poor food served in Stewards Hall. Bonham and six other South Carolinians died defending the Alamo in the battle with Mexican troops.

Who are the two alumni who received Medals of Honor?

Richmond H. Hilton, class of 1924. During World War I, Hilton led an attack on a German machine-gun nest, advancing well ahead of his men and personally killing six and capturing ten of the enemy soldiers. The wounds he received in this action resulted in the loss of an arm.

Kyle Carpenter, class of 2017. In Afghanistan, in support of Operation Enduring Freedom, in 2010, Carpenter used his own body to shield a fellow Marine from a grenade blast. He saved his fellow Marine but was severely wounded. After his medical retirement from the Marine Corps, Carpenter attended the University of South Carolina and graduated in 2017.

Which alumnus gave a free concert to USC students after the women's basketball team won its second national championship in 2022?

Grammy Award winner and country music artist Darius Rucker, lead singer of Hootie and the Blowfish.

Who is the donor of the largest gift in university history?

Darla Moore, class of 1975, donated $45 million to the business school in 2004, the largest gift in the university's history. Her previous gift of $25 million in 1998 was, at that time, the school's largest. Her total $70 million was the largest private gift to a business school in the United States.

Who was the first Black woman to enroll at the university?

Henri Monteith, in 1963.

Who was the first Black woman to graduate from USC?

Henri Monteith, in 1965.

> "My grandmother, Hattie Rakes, grew up in this area, actually four blocks from the governor's mansion to be exact. When she was a child, she couldn't even walk on the grounds of the University of South Carolina. She would have to walk around the campus just to get to where she needed to go. If only she was here today to see that the same grounds she had to walk around now is the same grounds that houses a statue of her granddaughter."
> —A'ja Wilson, 2021

Which alumnus was expelled for his antiwar activism?

Brett Bursey was a key figure in the antiwar movement at the university in the late 1960s and early 1970s. Bursey was arrested for protesting President Richard Nixon at the airport, for burning a Confederate flag on the Horseshoe, and for vandalizing the Richland County Selective Service Office in 1970. He was expelled and banned from campus.

Which alumna started a women's health hotline on campus while still an undergraduate?

Victoria Eslinger, class of 1969, law class of 1973, was a leading figure in the women's movement on campus. While an undergraduate, she set up a hotline that provided information on birth control and helped pregnant students obtain access to safe abortions out of state. As a law student, she sued to become the first female page at the South Carolina State House.

Which alumnus helped found the African American Studies Program?

Luther Battiste, class of 1971, lobbied for and coauthored the proposal to establish an African American Studies Program during his junior year. The program was established in 1971. Battiste also served as the campaign manager for Harry Walker, the first African American student body president, and helped found the first African American fraternity at USC, Kappa Alpha Psi, in 1970.

Which alumnus was known for writing songs about life at the antebellum college?

James R. Chalmers, class of 1851, was known for penning poems and songs about campus life. The favorite of his fellow students was a drinking song, "Billy Maybin's Oh!" The inn owned by Billy Maybin was a favorite hangout for South Carolina College students sneaking off campus in search of food, drinks, and a jovial atmosphere.

Which alumni won Pulitzer Prizes?

Jim Hoagland, class of 1961, won two Pulitzers, both while working for the *Washington Post*. The first was for international reporting in 1971 for his coverage of the fight against apartheid in South Africa; the second was for commentary in 1991 for his columns on the events leading to the Gulf War and for Mikhail Gorbachev's political problems.

Win McNamee, class of 1985, and Josh Dawsey, Class of 2012, were both part of teams that won Pulitzers in journalism in 2022 for their coverage of the January 6, 2021, assault on the US Capitol. McNamee won with fellow Getty Images photographers in the breaking news photography category. Dawsey won with fellow *Washington Post* journalists in the public service category.

Which alumnus was famous for hunting down gangsters in the 1930s?

FBI agent Melvin Purvis, law class of 1925, led the manhunts that captured or killed infamous bank robbers and gangsters, including John Dillinger, Pretty Boy Floyd, and Baby Face Nelson. His own fame made him a popular subject for Hollywood movies.

 **LEADERS**

Who proposed that a state-funded college should be founded in South Carolina?
Governor John Drayton.

Who was Carolina's longest-serving president?
Jonathan Maxcy was the first and the longest-serving president in university history. He led the school for sixteen years, from 1804 until his death in 1820.

Which Carolina president was described by a student as resembling "a wedge with a head on it"?
Thomas Cooper, second president of South Carolina College.

Who described out-of-state collectors of South Carolina historic materials as "literary bootleggers from outlandish parts"?
J. Rion McKissick, who was instrumental in establishing the South Caroliniana Library in order to keep historic materials in the Palmetto State.

Who was the first provost of the university?
William H. Patterson. The position was created in 1961.

Who was the first president to suggest building a brick wall around the campus and why?
Jonathan Maxcy suggested the construction of a brick wall, not to keep people off the campus but to try to keep the students on the campus and away from trouble in the city.

Which trustee led a drunken parade in the streets of Columbia with a drum and a fiddle?
Joseph Alston, as described by South Carolina College tutor Edward Hooker in his diary.

What course was Thomas Cooper famous for?
Political economy, which was one of the first—and possibly *the* first—course of that type in America. He was considered a pioneer in the subject, and his course and writings greatly influenced the students' political views, earning him the nickname the "Schoolmaster of States Rights."

Who had the shortest tenure as president?
Charles F. McCay, eighteen months, from December 1855 to May 1857.

Who was the first director of student activities?

James Driver, in 1924. The position included oversight of athletics at the time, as the board of trustees slowly took over control of football after virtually ignoring intercollegiate athletics since their beginning. This was an effort to pull control away from the influence of the alumni.

What secret came out after President Melton's death?

After President William Melton died unexpectedly in 1926, numerous students came forward to reveal that Melton had quietly and generously provided them with "loans" so that they could afford to go to college. The loans were actually personal gifts out of his own pocket, and the only condition was that they did not tell anyone.

Who served as acting president three times?

Leonard T. Baker was called upon more times than anyone else in the university's history to lead it through difficult times. The dean of the university was asked to serve as acting president on three different occasions—1926 to 1927, 1931 to 1932, and 1944 to 1945—each time after the death of the president. He served officially as president from 1932 to 1936. Upon his retirement in 1946, he was named Carolina's first president emeritus.

How many presidents died while in office?
Four. Jonathan Maxcy, William D. Melton, Davison M. Douglas, and J. Rion McKissick.

When was the university news service founded?
McKissick established the university news service to provide accurate information to the public in his effort to combat negative views about the university.

Who is the only person to have served nonconsecutive terms as president?
John M. McBryde is the only person who has served as Carolina's president in nonconsecutive terms (excluding persons who served as acting president). He was president from 1882 to 1883, and again from 1888 to 1891.

Which president introduced written exams?
The college had used oral exams since opening in 1805. President James Thornwell directed the switch to written ones in the 1850s.

Which president was nicknamed "Old Coot"?
Students nicknamed Thomas Cooper "Old Coot" because they thought he was shaped like a cooter, or a river turtle.

Who was the first woman provost?
Joan Gabel, from 2015 to 2019.

Who was the first African American provost?
William F. Tate IV, from 2020 to 2021.

How did President Samuel Chiles Mitchell fall into conflict with politicians and business leaders?
Mitchell had to curtail his speaking engagements on progressive subjects like Prohibition and child labor legislation because it could hurt the university politically by antagonizing powerful mill owners and anti-Prohibitionists. Mitchell also shocked white South Carolinians when he spoke at African American meetings and in African American churches.

Which governor publicly announced he was determined to drive President Mitchell out of the university?
Coleman Blease had a personal vendetta against the progressive Mitchell that included vicious racial overtones due to Mitchell's willingness to hold speaking engagements for African Americans. His attacks on Mitchell and the university eventually led to Mitchell's resignation in 1913. Mitchell then became president of the Medical College of Virginia.

Which president initiated the push for faculty to hold PhDs?
In 1923, only one-fourth of Carolina's faculty had PhDs. President Melton implemented the policy of giving preference to new faculty hires with that advanced degree. Longtime faculty pushed back, and history professor Yates Snowden wrote a poem criticizing the growing academic pressure for faculty to hold PhDs.

Who was the first registrar?

Alvin L. Wells, in 1922. The position brought considerable improvement to the management of grades, academic records, and transcripts.

Which president has been described as "the right man for the right time"?

Under Donald Russell's leadership, the university experienced a kind of renaissance with growth in its physical plant, a reorganization and strengthening of its academic programs, and a revitalization of the Carolina spirit after the postwar doldrum. Russell had wide-ranging success and a lengthy career. He held important positions in the Franklin D. Roosevelt administration during World War II, practiced law in South Carolina, and served as University of South Carolina president, governor, US senator, and federal judge.

Who hosted the senior dinners at the President's House?

The Russells were the first family to live in the renovated President's House. They wanted their home to be a welcoming place for students and faculty, so they hosted senior dinners. Each year, they invited every Carolina senior to dine with them at least once in the President's House.

Who were the university's first African American trustees?

Frances Lewis Cardozo and Benjamin A. Boseman, in 1868.

Which two presidents were known for riding their bicycles around campus?

J. Rion McKissick, president from 1936 to 1944, and Andrew Sorensen, president from 2002 to 2008.

President J. Rion McKissick riding the bicycle presented to him by the student body circa 1940. Courtesy of the University of South Carolina Archives.

Which president was known for impromptu speeches to the "Men and Women of Carolina"?

J. Rion McKissick often called students over to the Maxcy Monument or climbed atop a cafeteria table to address students.

Which president focused on bringing the university increased international visibility?

James B. Holderman was the dynamic, controversial president from 1977 to 1990. He brought USC increased international visibility, which included a foreign exchange agreement with Shanxi University in China—the first ever between an American university and a Chinese provincial university. Under his administration, private giving to the university increased, and the South Carolina Honors College was established. He also brought a multitude of national and international leaders and celebrities to the campus, including Pope John Paul II and Ronald Reagan. Holderman resigned after being investigated for improper use of university funds.

Which president worked on the response to the Three Mile Island nuclear accident in 1979?

John M. Palms, a nuclear physicist, was cohead of the response team who designed the public-assisted Ecological Based Environmental Radiation Monitoring Programs after the accident to monitor the effects of radiation in the area. He served as president of USC from 1991 to 2002.

Which president is buried on the Horseshoe?

J. Rion McKissick was one of the most popular presidents in school history, guiding the institution through the close of the Great Depression and World War II. His sudden death in 1944 shocked the university community. The students successfully petitioned the board of trustees to have their beloved president interred on campus, and McKissick was laid to rest in front of the west wing of the South Caroliniana Library on the Horseshoe—the only person ever to receive the honor.

What was the "bow tie tour"?

When Andrew Sorensen became president of the university in 2002, he decided to drive around the state to reach out to small communities. Since he was known for wearing bow ties, it became known as the "bow tie tour."

"Education is not a special privilege to be enjoyed by a favored few. I grow weary of the expression so often on the lips of men who call themselves educators that too many men and women go to college. However true this may be in other states, I believe that in South Carolina at least we have demonstrated that too few of our citizens have been given the advantage of a college education."
—President William Melton, 1925

Who was the first African American librarian?

In addition to teaching, Richard T. Greener served as the school's first African American librarian for nine months. During that time, he worked to reorganize and catalog the library's holdings, which were in disarray after the Civil War.

Who was president during the tumultuous events in the 1960s and 1970s?

Thomas F. Jones, one of the longest-serving presidents, oversaw a period of tremendous growth at the university. During his administration from 1962 to 1974, enrollment had more than tripled, and twenty-nine new buildings had been added to the campus. Jones also led the school during the desegregation of the university and dealt with the student activism of the 1970s.

Who managed the university's expansion in the 1960s and 1970s?

Carolina faced a student housing crisis in the 1960s due to rapidly increasing enrollment. Dean of Operations Harold Brunton managed the necessary building boom in the 1960s and 1970s, which included Capstone, Patterson Hall and South Tower, Gambrell and the Humanities complex, the Honeycombs, and the Carolina Coliseum.

Who led the student affairs division for nearly forty years?

Dennis Pruitt became head of the division in 1983. Under his leadership, Carolina became well known for its superior student experience. He retired in 2023.

TOWN AND GOWN

What is the original name of the University of South Carolina?

South Carolina College.

How many times has the institution been named/renamed?

Seven.

1801–1865	South Carolina College
1865–1880	University of South Carolina
1880–1882	South Carolina College of Agriculture and Mechanical Arts
1882–1887	South Carolina College
1887–1890	University of South Carolina
1890–1905	South Carolina College
1905–	University of South Carolina

On what date did the South Carolina Legislature establish South Carolina College?

December 19, 1801.

When did South Carolina College open?

Classes at South Carolina College began on January 10, 1805.

How many degrees were offered at South Carolina College?

Only one, the bachelor of arts. The curriculum focused on classical studies, including Greek and Latin.

How many faculty and students were there when it opened?

Two faculty members (including the president) and nine students.

How many were in the first graduating class in 1806?

Only one, Anderson Crenshaw.

When did Carolina first offer more than one degree?

The institution reopened after the Civil War in 1866 as the University of South Carolina with professional schools in law and medicine.

Why was South Carolina College founded?

It was an effort to unite the young men and future leaders from different areas of the state in order to promote "the good order and harmony of the state."

What connection did the founding of South Carolina College have to US president Thomas Jefferson?

It was part of Jefferson's Southern public college movement to establish colleges in each state.

How long did it take to establish South Carolina College?

Less than one month. Governor Drayton sent his proposal for the college to the legislature on November 23, 1801, and the "Act to Establish a College at Columbia" passed on December 19, 1801.

What was the first president's salary?

$2,500.

What were the first faculty salaries?

$1,000 to 1,500.

What budget did the legislature provide in 1805?

$6,000.

How was the hiring process for the president and faculty different in 1801?

The trustees considered names of people they were interested in, elected them to a position, and only then communicated with them to see if they were interested in the job.

Who were the first two faculty members?

President Jonathan Maxcy and Professor Enoch Hanford.

What was the minimum age requirement when South Carolina College opened?

Fourteen.

Were graduate degrees awarded prior to the Civil War?

Yes, but there were no set degree programs for them. A faculty member would simply set a course of study for each student.

When did the school open after the Civil War?

January 10, 1866, with seven faculty and forty-nine students, the anniversary of its original opening. The bill that reorganized the college into the first University of South Carolina was enacted on December 19, 1865, the anniversary of its original founding.

What is on the university's seal?

Beneath the university's motto stands the figures of Liberty and Minerva, the goddess of wisdom.

"The friendships of young men would thence be promoted and strengthened throughout the State, and our political union be much advanced thereby."
—Governor John Drayton, proposal to establish South Carolina College, 1801

What is the university mace?

The mace is carried on important occasions such as commencements, convocations, and formal dedications. Placing the mace on its stand signals the proceedings are about to begin, and the retirement of the mace signals the conclusion. The mace was officially adopted in 1967. It was presented to the university by alumnus Dr. George Curry, as a memorial to Susan Richardson Guignard. It was designed and crafted by distinguished London silversmith Leslie Durbin. The mace's head includes the seals of the university, the state of South Carolina, and the Great Seal of the United States. A palmetto tree rises from the middle of the seals; its fronds are formed by a group of thirteen stars, representing the founding colonies. The eight stars on the shaft are an homage to South Carolina as the eighth state to join the Union.

How many universities are in the University of South Carolina system?

Eight: Columbia, Aiken, Beaufort, Lancaster, Salkehatchie, Sumter, Union, and Upstate.

How many degree programs does the university currently offer?

More than 350.

What economic impact does the university have on South Carolina?

USC is a major economic driver in the state, contributing $6.2 billion a year to the economy and supporting more than sixty-three thousand jobs statewide.

How did enrollment figures change between 1940 and 2022?

In 1940, 2,004 students were enrolled. In 2022, 51,411 students were enrolled systemwide, including 30,661 women, 7,186 African Americans, and 2,031 international students.

How many degrees were awarded in 1806? In 2022?

1806—one
2022—12,436

What was the tuition in 1805? In 2022?

1805—$20 per year
2022—$12,668 for residents; $34,934 for nonresidents

When were women admitted to the university?

The state legislature passed a law in 1893 that required women to be allowed to enroll. The first women enrolled in 1895 as nondegree-seeking students.

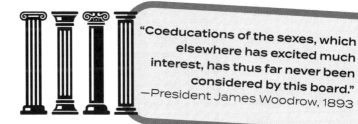

"Coeducations of the sexes, which elsewhere has excited much interest, has thus far never been considered by this board."
—President James Woodrow, 1893

How did the administration and male students react to coeducation?

University administrators, faculty, and many students did not want the institution to become coeducational. Restrictions were placed on women's admission, and they were not provided with a residence hall or even an adequate restroom. Continued hostility kept the number of women low until World War I. In 1908, there were only ten women out of 298 students. Many women inquired about attending the university but could not attend due to the lack of residence halls.

Which governor recommended women to be allowed to attend South Carolina College?

Benjamin Tillman, in 1893.

What group was referred to as a "Monstrous Regiment?"

The first women admitted to the university.

Why did Carolina try to merge with a women's college?

In 1913, the university worked to circumvent the coeducation requirement via merger with the College for Women in Columbia. An official merger of the two institutions would be similar to the Radcliffe and Harvard model—it would solve the financial problems of the women's college and allow women to get degrees from the University of South Carolina but at a separate campus. There was positive support in the legislature, but the proposal was derailed due to the original charter of the women's school stating the property had to be used for "distinctly Christian education of young women."

When was the university desegregated?

Carolina was desegregated twice, first during Reconstruction from 1873 to 1877, and again in 1963.

How was it desegregated in 1873?

The state constitution of 1868 called for the integration of all of South Carolina's state-supported schools. It was the first time the university was open to all South Carolina men, regardless of race. By 1873, the board of trustees, the faculty, and the student body were all desegregated.

How did the white faculty and students react?

Faculty members resigned their positions, and students quit the institution.

> **"We propose to stay, and to show the masculine portion of the students that Providence did not give the greater portion of mind to them."**
> —Beulah G. Calvo, in response to hostile atmosphere toward women students, 1897

Did other Southern universities also integrate during Reconstruction?

The University of South Carolina was the only state-supported Southern university to integrate during the Reconstruction era that followed the Civil War.

Why did desegregation end in 1877?

When Reconstruction ended in 1877, and Confederate general Wade Hampton was elected governor, the legislature closed the university. It was reorganized and reopened in 1880 as an all-white institution again.

When was the first time African American women were able to attend school on the Carolina campus?

During Reconstruction, the legislature passed a bill that created the State Normal School for Teachers. Although the normal school was not affiliated with the university, it was housed in Rutledge College and the old president's house, and university professors provided lectures. Its student body was almost entirely African American women.

Students and teacher of the Normal School circa 1874.
Courtesy of the University of South Carolina Archives.

What is a normal school?

The term "normal" refers to the goal of teaching the practice or "norms" of pedagogy (teaching).

When was the second desegregation?

On September 11, 1963, the first three African American students since Reconstruction registered for classes at the University of South Carolina. The university had fought attempts at desegregation for decades, but when the courts made clear it was inevitable, the administration worked with city and state officials to make sure that the campus wasn't marred by the violence occurring at other Southern universities. The university erected a low fence around parts of the campus to help control any protestors, and the South Carolina Army National Guard conducted riot-control exercises. President Thomas Jones issued a public statement that the university would not tolerate disturbances.

Who were the students?

Undergraduates Robert Anderson and Henri Monteith, and graduate student James Solomon, registered for classes in Hamilton College and answered media questions. The university's plans for a peaceful desegregation worked so well that the day received little coverage from the national media, prompting a newspaper editor to comment that no violence apparently meant no coverage. As undergraduates living on campus, however, Monteith and Anderson were subjected to racial hostility. Anderson, in particular, was targeted with threats of violence.

When did they graduate?

Monteith graduated in 1965, the first African American woman ever to do so. Anderson graduated in 1966. Solomon, who already held a master's degree from Atlanta University, enrolled in courses but did not pursue a degree.

When did Phi Beta Kappa establish a chapter at Carolina?

In 1926.

What was the top vocation of students' parents in 1940?

Farming.

How much did enrollment and state revenue change between the world wars?

Between World War I (1918) and World War II (1941), enrollment jumped from 386 students to two thousand. The percentage of revenue provided by the state legislature dropped from 90 percent in 1918 to 54 percent in 1941. Today, enrollment is around fifty thousand students, and the state provides around 11 to 12 percent of the university's budget.

Name the top five states (besides South Carolina) with the highest enrollment at the University of South Carolina.

North Carolina, Georgia, New Jersey, New York, and Virginia.

Name the top five countries (besides the United States) with the highest enrollment at the University of South Carolina.

China, India, Republic of Korea, Bangladesh, and Germany.

Did any faculty and staff serve in World War II?

Forty-two members of the faculty and staff were granted leaves of absence from their jobs to take part in the war.

How many alumni served in World War II?

It is estimated that more than six thousand alumni of the university served in all branches of the armed forces.

What did students do to support the war effort during World War II?

Students served as firefighters, air raid spotters, and first aid helpers in the campus civil defense program and formed a Red Cross chapter on campus.

What board of trustees' proposal in 1944 caused a statewide uproar?

With the campus needing major expansion but hemmed in by Columbia businesses and neighborhoods, the board approved a plan conceived by trustee and South Carolina speaker of house Solomon Blatt to move the university to a new location at the edge of Columbia. The plan set off a firestorm of protest from faculty, students, and alumni across the state, as well as business leaders in the downtown area. Ultimately, Blatt withdrew the proposal.

Why was a chemical engineering laboratory housed in an old firehouse in 1946?

The influx of veterans enrolling in the university post–World War II left the university scrambling for classroom spaces and forcing it to use basements, attics, garages, and the old fire station on Main Street.

Who described out-of-state manuscript collectors as "literary bootleggers from outlandish parts"?

President McKissick was instrumental in transforming the original library building into the South Caroliniana Library, citing the need to prevent the state's historical materials from falling into the collections in other states.

Name the university's first regional campus.

The university established its first regional campus in Florence, in the basement of the public library, in 1957. It moved to a permanent campus in 1961. In 1970, it broke away from Carolina to become Francis Marion University.

Name the second regional campus that split from the university.

Originally a junior college branch of the College of Charleston from 1954 to 1958, Coastal Carolina became a regional campus of the University of South Carolina in 1960. It became an independent university in 1993.

What is the Palmetto College?

It consists of the university's associate degree-granting campuses (Lancaster, Salkehatchie, Sumter, and Union) and online bachelor's degree completion programs.

When was the alma mater written and by whom?

In 1911, by English professor George A. Wauchope. It is set to Robert Burns's "Flow Gently, Sweet Afton."

What is the proper way to raise your hand at the end of the alma mater?

With your hand raised as if you are holding up a glass in a toast.

What famous person slept on the floor of the President's House guest room?

When Senator (and future US president) John F. Kennedy visited the campus to give the commencement speech in 1957, Virginia Russell asked him if she could do anything to make his visit more comfortable. Kennedy had a bad back and requested that a board be placed under the mattress. A three-quarter-inch piece of plywood was placed under the mattress, but the following morning she learned from the housekeeper that Kennedy had moved the linens to the floor and slept there.

Which president's family had a menagerie of pets?

Thomas Jones's family had a wide variety of pets, including several birds. His daughter Cissie's blue jay, Vida, lived in the President's House, eating and drinking from Mary Jones's plate and glass. Vida also had a habit of carrying off Mrs. Jones's earrings and stashing them on top of the window drapes. Vida, Jerry the parakeet, and Boris the sparrow liked to try to ride around on female guests' bouffant hairdos. Cissie bought Rusty the gamecock as a Christmas gift for President Jones one year. The rooster had a garnet and black harness and could be taken for walks, and occasionally went to football games.

What future president gave the university's 1957 commencement address?

John F. Kennedy.

What was notable about the Class of 1906?

As freshmen, they entered the South Carolina College, but they were the first group of students to graduate from the current University of South Carolina.

Who was the first sitting US president to visit the campus?

In 1909, William Howard Taft became the first sitting US president to visit the campus. He stood on the steps of the original president's house to speak to the large crowd of faculty, students, and Columbia residents gathered on the Horseshoe.

When was the College of Arts and Sciences established?

In 1912. It was split into different colleges in the 1970s (Arts and Letters, Social and Behavioral Sciences, and Science and Mathematics) before eventually all merging back together in 2004 into its current form.

"The university is the focal point for educational progress in our state. ... If you want to build education, you have to start with the college."
—President Donald S. Russell, 1952

Why did USC hold an elaborate Shakespearean Pageant in 1916?

The university and Columbia communities held a joint commemoration of the three hundredth anniversary of Shakespeare's death that had a cast of nine hundred costumed participants, including faculty and students. Two performances were held: a London May Day in Elizabethan England, on the Horseshoe, and an evening costume ball at which scenes from Shakespeare's plays were performed. Two thousand spectators attended the events.

When was the School of Business established?

The university established a School of Commerce in 1919. It included a Secretarial Science Program that initially attracted most of the women students in the school. By the 1940s, however, the secretarial courses were dropped and the name changed to School of Business Administration. In 1998, Carolina became the first major university to name its business school for a woman when it was named for alumna and benefactor Darla Moore.

How did World War I affect the university?

When America entered World War I in 1917, a Reserve Officer Training Corps unit was quickly established at Carolina. It was the first time that military training had returned to the campus since before the Civil War. By the fall of 1917, three-fourths of the student body joined the ROTC. The university also adjusted its curriculum to meet the demands for certain types of training, including the addition of Red Cross courses.

Did many faculty serve in the war effort?

The war seriously crippled Carolina's teaching effectiveness. By the fall of 1918, almost half of the faculty members had been released from their teaching duties so they could serve in the armed forces or perform other war-related service.

How did World War II affect the university?

Carolina adjusted its curriculum to support the war effort, including establishing a nursing degree program in 1944, and reassigning faculty members to teach navigation, mathematics, and communications in the Navy's programs.

Why did the campus resemble a naval base in 1943?

Carolina became home to a Naval Reserve Officer Training Corps unit and three US Naval programs, which more than made up for the drop in civilian enrollment. The university again adjusted its curriculum, and it operated on a twelve-month basis from 1943 until August 1945, with no holidays other than Christmas.

"It is wonderful to be young, it is wonderful to be a student in the university, it is wonderful to be young and a student at the University of South Carolina."
—Pope John Paul II, September 11, 1987

What time period is referred to as the Carolina Renaissance?

During his administration from 1952 to 1957, President Donald Russell put much of his energy into improving the basic sciences at USC, which had been suffering from inadequate facilities and a lack of properly trained faculty. Course offerings, facilities, and equipment were upgraded, and Russell recruited an outstanding faculty to beef up the science programs. He also brought nationally prominent figures to the campus and initiated the development of an international studies program. Russell breathed fresh life into the institution and put it on the path to becoming a modern research university.

When was the College of Pharmacy established?

It was established in 1888 but closed in 1891. However, classes continued to be offered. It was reestablished as a school in 1925.

Why did former secretary of state Henry Kissinger visit the campus?

Kissinger was among the international diplomats that attended a North Atlantic Treaty Organization conference on the future of the Western Alliance, hosted by the university in the 1980s.

When did Ronald Reagan visit the university?

Ronald Reagan's visit in 1983 was the first time the university awarded an honorary degree to an incumbent chief executive. After the ceremony, Reagan was presented with a USC sweatshirt and cap. Reagan returned to the University for a Caribbean conference in 1984.

What was the Ecumenical Year?

In 1986-87, the university sponsored an Ecumenical Year that brought world religious leaders to the campus—Greek Orthodox Archbishop Iakovos, the Reverend Billy Graham, the Archbishop of Canterbury, and Pope John Paul II.

What did Carolina students chant to welcome the pope?

"John Paul Two, we love you!"

How did the pope respond?

"John Paul Two, he loves you!"

Pope John Paul II speaks to students on the Horseshoe, September 11, 1987. Courtesy of the University of South Carolina Archives.

How many people crowded onto the Horseshoe to see the pope?

More than ten thousand.

What slogan was printed on T-shirts for the pope's visit?

"I was moved by the pope." They were given to the students who had to vacate their Horseshoe dormitories for the pope's visit.

Where did the pope conduct a service of Christian worship?

At Williams-Brice Stadium for more than sixty thousand people.

What South Carolina governor tried to close the university?

Benjamin R. Tillman, who was instrumental in the founding of Clemson Agricultural College and who campaigned against the "elite" of the state, said USC was the "seedbed of the aristocracy."

When was the law school established?

In 1867.

How many degrees were awarded during the Reconstruction university?

Twenty-eight degrees were awarded during those four years—fourteen bachelors of arts and fourteen bachelors of law.

Did the university have a service flag during World War I?
Yes, with more than five hundred blue stars representing the alumni serving in the war.

When was the PhD program established?
In 1923.

When did USC officially adopt a flag?
In 1976. It has the university's seal in a field of garnet and black, designed as part of USC 175th celebrations.

What was the PhB and how many has Carolina awarded?
Charles Babbitt was the only person to ever be awarded the bachelor of philosophy at Carolina.

When did Carolina have a farm?
When the institution was reorganized as the College of Agriculture and Mechanics in 1880, a twenty-acre farm was created in the area that includes present day Davis Field, and the sites of Russell House and women's quad. It was later enlarged with an additional forty acres rented on South Pickens Street. The farm grew cotton, corn, oats, and other crops.

Why are the school colors garnet and black?
The origins are unknown, but the colors have always been associated with Carolina's teams beginning with the 1892 Furman football game.

What was the Extension Division?

The Extension Division's purpose was to take the university into the community, thereby "extending the usefulness of the university." It primarily offered correspondence courses at first, then developed public service programs including faculty lectures, teaching aids, home reading courses, and an information bureau. Its high school program included statewide scholastic speaking and athletic contests. The department was the initial step to establishing the system campuses.

Why is the College of Hospitality, Retail, and Sport Management the most reorganized and renamed school at Carolina?

Its roots go back to the Extension Division in 1915, before it went through eight different reorganizations and name changes, morphing from General Studies in 1962 to its current form.

When did Carolina start using standardized entrance exams?

In 1954, the university was the first state-supported institution in the Southeast to require entrance exams in addition to high school diplomas.

When was the South Carolina Honors College established?

In 1977.

When was the School of Public Health established?

In 1974. It was renamed the Arnold School of Public Health in 2001, after Norman J. and Gerry Sue Arnold, who donated $10 million to support the school's work in research, teaching, and public education.

When did the LLB become the JD?

The change was due to a nationwide shift in law schools from undergraduates to primarily graduate students. By 1971, the bachelor of law was replaced by the professional degree of juris doctor.

How did the 1918 influenza pandemic affect Carolina?

The campus had to be quarantined since one-third of the university's students got sick. The students included members of the War Department's Student Army Training Corps. A captain of one of the companies, Gadsden Shand, had to take care of his fellow trainees. Shand was just sixteen years old. The administration turned Woodrow College and the gymnasium (now Longstreet Theatre) into makeshift flu wards. Six of the student trainees died, but all of the members of Shand's company survived.

"Learning humanizes character and does not permit it to be cruel."
—University of South Carolina motto

Where were the three memorials to World War I alumni placed?

In April 1919, memorial trees were planted on Greene and Pickens Streets in honor of the twenty-eight students and alumni who died during the Mexican border dispute and World War I. Granite and stone markers were added at the base of the trees later. A marker was placed on the front of South Caroliniana Library, and in 1927 the American Legion placed granite boulder with a marker on Greene Street near Petigru College.

When was the Graduate School established?

It was set up as a department in 1906 and given the title of school in 1907, but requirements for graduate degrees were still vague until its reorganization in 1923 when the PhD program was established.

When was the School of Journalism and Mass Communications established?

In 1923, as the School of Journalism. It became the College of Journalism and Mass Communications in 1987, then changed from College to School in 2002.

When was the School of Library and Information Science established?

In 1972, as the College of Librarianship. It was renamed College of Library and Information Science in 1982, then School of Library and Information Science in 2002.

When did the Journalism and Library Schools merge?

The two schools merged under one umbrella in 2002 and are now the College of Information and Communication.

When was the College of Nursing established?

In 1957, the department of nursing was pulled from the College of Arts and Sciences and expanded into a full four-year school. A new, centralized facility was constructed in 1975, through a significant bequest by the late Martha Williams Brice. The building was named in honor of the Williams and Brice families.

When was the College of Social Work established?

In 1934, though it was discontinued in 1953, and then reestablished in 1969.

When was the College of Education established?

It was first established as the Normal School, from 1888 to 1891. After several name changes, it became the College of Education in 1971.

When did the university first award degrees in the summer?

In 1927.

When was the School of Medicine established?

The first medical school was operated from 1867 to 1876. The current school was established in 1974, and the first classes were held in 1977.

When was the university unable to pay its faculty?

During the Great Depression, the university's budget situation became so dire that it had to issue faculty salaries in scrip instead of cash. Scrip is a legal substitute for money that has to be redeemed by the employer issuing it. Most of the scrip was redeemed by 1933 but some was not until 1945.

How did the University of South Carolina benefit from US president Franklin Delano Roosevelt's New Deal programs?

The first funds from the New Deal came in 1934 with a Civil Works Administration grant to make general repairs to several buildings on campus and add sidewalks on Sumter, Green, and College Streets.

What buildings were constructed from New Deal funding?

Maxcy, Preston, Sims, McKissick, and Longstreet's natatorium (swimming pool).

How were students helped by the New Deal?

Work scholarships were established in 1934 from the Federal Emergency Relief Administration and from the National Youth Administration at $15 per month.

What kind of entertainment could students participate in during the depression?

Students still found ways to entertain themselves through activities like Main Street movie theaters, bowling, milkshakes at Burnett's drug store, and playing piano in the women's dormitory lounge.

When was the University of South Carolina press established?

In 1944.

Who was Literary Bob?

Longtime African American custodian Robert Herrin gained the nickname "Literary Bob" due to his extensive knowledge of the library collections. In the early 1900s, less than half the books were cataloged, and Herrin was the only person who knew where they all were. The librarian at that time had little professional training.

Who was USC's first Rhodes Scholar?

William Henry Verner, in 1900.

How many Rhodes Scholars has USC had?

Ten.

When was the School of Music established?

In 1994, seventy years after music was added as a department.

When was the College of Engineering and Computing established?

In 1909, as the School of Engineering. In 1999, it merged with computer sciences under its current name.

Why did a student hand President Andrew Sorensen a bag of sugar at commencement?

A group of students had borrowed a cup of sugar from the Sorensens one evening. Two years later, one of the students handed him a bag of sugar as she walked across the stage at commencement and thanked him for the loan.

What was "The USC" campaign?

As part of his campaign to raise the national and international profile of the university, President James Holderman introduced the usage of "The USC," because the University of South Carolina was the first USC to be founded. Usage of "SC" and "South Carolina" were dropped, to the dismay of alumni.

Why did Carolina lose the right to trademark the interlocking script of "SC?"

The University of Southern California sued the University of South Carolina in 2006 over the use of the interlocking "SC" logo. Even though the interlocking "SC" was brought back in the 1990s, Carolina lost the right to trademark it because the courts determined that it had "abandoned the mark" during the 1980s. Carolina can still use the logo, but without the trademark, it can't control who else uses it.

> "Oh, they got deathly sick, and the amazing part about it was, it all happened in one day. All of them. Except two of us."
> —Gadsden Shand on the 1918 influenza pandemic, 1998

Why did Southern Cal sue over this?

Southern Cal, which uses an interlocking maroon and gold block "SC" for its athletic teams, argued fans would be confused by the similarity with South Carolina's interlocking garnet and black script "SC."

Aren't those different colors and styles and isn't Southern Cal on the opposite side of the country?

Yes.

CAMPUS

How large was the original campus?
The original quadrangle was twenty-four acres, and bounded by Sumter, Pendleton, Bull, and Devine Streets.

How large is the Columbia campus now?
444 acres.

How many buildings were on campus when South Carolina College opened in 1805?
One.

What was the first building?
Rutledge College. It contained student and faculty housing, a library, classrooms, a chapel, and laboratories. The building is named for brothers John and Edward Rutledge, both of whom served as governor of South Carolina.

Is there still a chapel?
Yes. Rutledge Chapel was renovated under the direction of President Donald Russell in the 1950s and rededicated as an interfaith chapel. The room features excellent acoustics and a European crystal chandelier imported by Donald and Virginia Russell.

What building was damaged by an earthquake?

DeSaussure College, constructed in 1809, was severely damaged by an earthquake in 1811 and had to be reinforced with iron rods.

What were the original names of DeSaussure and Rutledge?

North Building (DeSaussure) and South Building (Rutledge).

Did professors originally live on campus?

South Carolina College required faculty members to live on the campus and provided residences for them, most of which were duplexes. After the Civil War, that requirement was no longer in effect, but residences were still available for faculty members.

When did the university stop providing residences?

After World War II, campus faculty residences were converted into academic and administrative offices.

What were the original residences on the Horseshoe?

The original President's House, 1807 (demolished 1939)
First professor's house, 1810 (demolished 1854)
Second professor's house, 1813 (now McCutchen House)
Third professor's house, 1837 (now Lieber College)
Current President's House, 1854 (built originally as a
    professor's house)
Fourth professor's house, 1860 (now Flinn Hall)

Why was a brick wall built around the original campus?

A seven-foot-tall brick wall with only one entrance was constructed in 1835 and 1836 to replace the wooden barriers that surrounded the campus. Its purpose wasn't to keep people out, but to keep the students in. They liked to sneak off campus at night and engage in "ungentlemanly" behavior.

Why was it a big deal for students to leave campus back then?

Students were not allowed to leave campus without permission from the president or a professor, not even to visit relatives. They frequently did, however, sneak out to eat and drink at taverns, and to play pranks on Columbia residents.

Did the wall work?

The wall did not keep the students on campus. They found ways to climb over it and continue their nightly activities. It did, however, protect the campus from the flames that consumed much of the city on the night of February 17, 1865.

Are parts of the wall still there?

The wall still borders the old campus on Greene, Sumter, Pendleton Streets, and parts of Bull Street. Portions have been greatly altered over the years, but the sides on Pendleton and Greene Streets are the most original sections.

What was discovered in one of the bricks?

A condition survey of the wall conducted by historic preservation students in 2011 discovered that one of the slave-made bricks retained the impression of its maker's fingers. The brick was carefully removed during the renovation of the wall and placed in the collections of McKissick Museum.

When did the Horseshoe get its name?

The original campus didn't get its nickname until the 1890s, when the center entrance in the Sumter Street side of the brick wall was closed, and two entrances were created. This gave the driveway an upside-down U-shape in line with the layout of the buildings, and the Horseshoe name was born.

When was the President's House built?

Trick question! There have been two. The first was built in 1807. The second was built in 1855 but did not become the President's House until a century later.

Where was the first one?

The original president's residence was located at the head of the horse, between Rutledge and DeSaussure Colleges.

What happened to it?

The house served as the residence of every university president from Jonathan Maxcy to William S. Currell. President Melton refused to live there in 1922 because of its poor condition, so it was converted into offices. Despite its deteriorating condition, it continued to be used until part of the ceiling collapsed in 1937. It was demolished in 1939 during construction of a library, now McKissick Museum, which was built directly behind the old house.

Under the big trees at the head of the Horseshoe, there are two small, round brass markers dated 1807. To what do they refer?

They mark the front foundation corners of the original President's House.

Name the building that served as a federal military prison.

After the Civil War, when United States troops occupied the campus and the city of Columbia, they converted one wing of DeSaussure College into a military prison.

Which Horseshoe building was nearly torn down in the 1970s due to its poor condition?

McCutchen House, built in 1813, was in such poor condition in the 1970s that it was under consideration for demolition. However, its leaning walls and other issues were resolved, and the building was turned into a faculty club.

Is the faculty club still there?

No, the club operated at a loss for many years and closed in 2002.

What is in McCutchen House now?

McCutchen now houses the Culinary Institute at Carolina and food service laboratories for the School of Hotel, Restaurant, and Tourism Management. The restaurant is open to the public.

What structure is considered the most architecturally distinctive building on the Horseshoe?

The South Caroliniana Library.

South Caroliniana Library circa 1874. Courtesy of the University of South Carolina Archives.

What national distinction does the building have?

Constructed in 1840, the library is the oldest freestanding academic library in the United States. Prior to its construction, college and university libraries were housed in multipurpose buildings.

Who designed the building?

The most distinctive elements of the building were designed by nineteenth-century architect Robert Mills, a South Carolinian noted for his churches, courthouses, and homes across the South. Mills also served as the nation's first federal architect and designed several federal buildings, the most famous of which is the Washington Monument. Mills also designed Carolina's own Maxcy Monument.

What makes it so architecturally distinctive?

The reading room on the second floor is a near replica of an earlier reading room of the Library of Congress, with graceful columns, skylights, alcoves, an ornate ceiling, and large windows looking out onto the Horseshoe.

What does the name "South Caroliniana" mean?

Caroliniana is Latin for "things pertaining to Carolina." After serving as the campus library for one hundred years, the building's purpose was refocused on collecting published and unpublished materials relating to the history, literature, and culture of South Carolina, and it was named the South Caroliniana Library.

Is there really a Civil War cannonball on campus?

The cannonball and a defective marble column originally intended for use in the State House are on display in the garden of the South Caroliniana Library. After the building underwent major renovations in the late 1970s, the garden was also renovated. It features a three-tiered foundation donated by the American Revolution Centennial Richland County Committee, the Lucy Hampton Bostick Trust, and the University South Caroliniana Society. The garden was refreshed in 2023 with new plantings, including native species.

Does the university president still live on campus?

Yes. In the 1950s, President Donald S. Russell and his wife, Virginia Russell, directed the renovation of the vacant faculty duplex built in 1854 into the current President's House. All of the university's presidents have lived there since Russell and his family.

How many presidents have lived in the house since 1952?

Ten. Donald Russell, Robert Sumwalt, Thomas Jones, William Patterson, James Holderman, John Palms, Andrew Sorensen, Harris Pastides, Robert Caslen, and, currently, Michael Amaridis.

How many fireplaces were originally in the President's House?

Thirteen.

Who was the first president to live in the current President's House?

Trick question! J. Rion McKissick and his wife, Caroline Dick McKissick, moved into the eastern half of the faculty duplex in 1932 when he became dean of the School of Journalism. They remained in the house when he became president in 1936, until his death in 1944. Donald Russell was the first president to live there after it became the official president's residence.

Isn't there some special wallpaper in the house?

The Russells personally purchased antique furnishings for the residence, including a spectacular wallcovering in the second-floor reception room. Dated at approximately 1811, it was made in France and depicts a European fantasy style of a Chinese wedding. It was made by block printing, in which carved blocks were inked and pressed onto paper, which was pressed to a fabric backing.

Why was the fountain in the garden moved from its original location in front of the house?

When it was installed in front of the President's House in the 1960s, it quickly became a favorite spot for a student prank. Students liked to pour detergent in the fountain to produce great mounds of bubbles, to the amusement of President Thomas Jones and his wife, Mary. However, the following president, William Patterson, was not amused, and he had the fountain moved to the garden.

Besides the fountain, is there a special feature in the garden?

A Present Past, a fresco by alumna Taylor Tynes, is a prominent feature. The depictions of characters in the fresco are homages to art, philosophy, and education, and a reflection on the university's motto, "Learning humanizes character and does not permit it to be cruel." In addition to woodland creatures, Tynes included a nod to Mary Jones, wife of President Thomas Jones, in the form of a blue jay carrying a pearl earring. The Jones family had a pet blue jay that frequently hid her earrings.

What chair in the President's House is no one allowed to sit in?

The chair used by Pope John Paul II during his visit to the university on September 11, 1987, is on display outside the reception room. It was made for the pope's visit by Joseph S. Cjartoseki of Peconic, New York. With the canonization of Pope John Paul II to sainthood in 2014, the chair became a "relic of the second class," or an "authentic contact relic," which is an object touched by a saint in his or her lifetime.

What is the small brick building in the garden of the President's House?

It is the last remaining kitchen and slave quarters building on the campus. Because South Carolina College provided housing for its faculty and their families, the faculty were permitted to bring their own enslaved household workers. The kitchen occupied the first floor of the structure, and living quarters for the enslaved workers were on the second floor.

> "None of the buildings belonging to the University of South Carolina has a history which, for sheer frustration, compares with that of College Hall [Longstreet Theatre]."
> —historian Daniel Hollis, 1951

Did South Carolina College own enslaved persons?

South Carolina College owned a few enslaved persons but primarily relied on a hiring-out system, which allowed the college to temporarily hire enslaved workers from local businesses or residents. This system provided the school with a labor force while sparing it from many of the costs associated with owning slaves. Enslaved persons performed most of the labor on the campus, meal preparation, cleaning and grounds-keeping, and general maintenance and repair work. Some cleaned the library books and laboratory equipment.

Name the building that first housed women students.

The east wing of DeSaussure College became the first location for women's housing on campus in 1918, although women had been admitted to the University since 1895. When male students began leaving to join the armed forces for the Great War, the university allowed more women to enroll and provided their first residence hall.

Why was Longstreet Theatre considered an unlucky building?

The building seemed jinxed from the start. It was constructed in 1855 as a chapel and auditorium for South Carolina College, but its construction was completed two years late and its roof blew off twice. It was never able to be used as an auditorium because it suffered from terrible acoustics that could not be corrected, despite multiple efforts. It was later converted into a science facility in 1888, then into a gymnasium in 1893. Modern technology finally resolved the acoustics by converting it into a theatre-in-the-round in 1976.

Where were African American women first able to attend classes on campus?

Rutledge College and the old President's House. During Reconstruction, the university was desegregated from 1873 to 1877, but it was still all-male. The African American women were enrolled in a separate institution, the State Normal School for Teachers, which the University hosted in Rutledge College and the old President's House.

Name the first major building to be constructed after the Civil War.

Constructed in 1909, Davis College was the first new building on campus since before the Civil War. It's also the first university building constructed on Gibbes Green.

What is notable about Thornwell College?

When it was completed in 1913, Thornwell College was the first residence hall to be built at the university in sixty-five years.

Name the first building on campus to have central heating.

Built in 1914, Woodrow was the first dormitory with central heating. It was used as a hospital during the influenza epidemic of 1918.

What was the original name and use of Currell College?

Currell College was constructed in 1919 as the university's law school and was originally named after James Louis Petigru. The names under the windows commemorate noted South Carolina lawyers and judges. When a new law school building was constructed in 1950, the name Petigru was transferred to the new building and the old one was renamed for William Spenser Currell, president from 1914 to 1922.

Name the first residence hall constructed for women.

The original Wade Hampton dormitory, built in 1924, was the first women's residence hall. The building was demolished in 1959 and the current dorm was constructed in its place.

What happened to the campus during the Civil War?

The college was closed during the Civil War, and the Confederate authorities took over the campus for use as a hospital. All the academic buildings, except for the library, were pressed into use. Professors and their families were allowed to stay in their campus residences.

What campus building served as a morgue?

The basement of Longstreet Theatre served as the Confederate hospital morgue.

How many observatories has Carolina had on its campus?

Three. The first was built in 1817 behind a faculty residence. The second observatory was constructed in 1852 and is still standing between Thornwell College and Osborne Administration Building. It had a twelve-foot-diameter revolving dome with a seven-inch brass telescope. The telescope was reported stolen in 1867, probably for the brass. The building became a fraternity hall in 1884 and later served as storage. It currently serves as administrative offices.

The third, Melton Observatory, was built in 1928, on Greene Street. It was funded by what was, at that time, the largest gift ever given to the university by an alumnus—$15,000 from Edwin G. Siebels. The observatory has a sixteen-inch reflecting telescope. It was named for William Davis Melton, who served as president of the university from 1922 until his sudden death in 1926.

Why are there white brick initials in the Horseshoe sidewalks?

Until 1931, the Horseshoe had no sidewalks, because the state legislature would not provide funding. English professor Havilah Babcock, tired of trudging through the mud on rainy days, worked with student organizations and other faculty members to bring sidewalks to the 'Shoe. The project raised money and secured the assistance of local brick company Richland Shale for providing bricks and brick masons. The students laid the bricks themselves. The initials are the participating student organizations, and those of Professors Havilah Babcock and George A. Wauchope.

Why is there another set of initials in regular red bricks?

Those are the initials of African American brick mason Marion E. Evans, who worked on the project.

Did the university really have its own high school?

University High School was jointly established by the university and the Columbia Public Schools. It opened in 1932 and fulfilled the need for teaching-practice facilities for education majors. It closed in 1966.

What was the last building constructed prior to the Civil War?

A faculty residence built in 1860, now known as Flinn Hall, was the last building constructed prior to the Civil War.

Why is it in an odd location?

Flinn Hall was originally located at the corner of Sumter and Pendleton Streets. In 1910, it was named for Professor William Flinn, who had lived in the house. It served as the headquarters for the YMCA for many years. The building was moved back around fifty yards to its present location to allow for the construction of the War Memorial building at the corner of the campus.

What is the War Memorial building?

The World War Memorial Building is dedicated to the men and women of South Carolina who served and died in World War I. It was constructed in 1935 by the War Memorial Commission and the Historical Commission of South Carolina and funded by private subscription from South Carolinians and a federal grant from the Public Works Administration. University trustees allowed the building to be placed on the corner of Sumter and Pendleton Streets and decided to move Flinn Hall instead of demolishing it.

Who designed it?

Lafaye and Lafaye designed the building, which has numerous unique architectural features, including an exterior of Indiana limestone, bronze doors, text inscriptions in the walls, several kinds of marble in the building's interior including a marble altar, and Art Deco-influenced fixtures. The building's frieze is inscribed, "They were willing to die / for liberty and world peace / they strove that war might cease." The cornerstone of the building contains several items including a complete roster of the South Carolina men and women, white and black, who served in the armed forces in World War I.

How many buildings were originally on the campus?

Fourteen major buildings were constructed on the original campus grounds between 1805 and 1860. Eleven of them are still standing.

Were there other outbuildings?

In addition to the Maxcy Monument, there were numerous outbuildings, including outhouses, slave quarters, carriage houses, and sheds. They were gradually demolished in the early twentieth century as the university filled in those spaces with larger buildings.

What was the Horseshoe Restoration Project?

It was a decade-long renovation and restoration project for the Horseshoe buildings, from 1972 to 1982. The earliest impetus for the project occurred in 1972, when a shower stall in one of the men's residence halls on the Horseshoe fell through a rotted floor. Fortunately, the shower wasn't occupied at the time. The approaching United States bicentennial also brought support for the project.

How much did it cost?

Over a period of ten years, and at an expense of more than $10 million, the Horseshoe's buildings were restored as much as possible to their appearance prior to 1860.

When were the iron gates added to the Horseshoe entrance?

The wrought iron gates were donated by the Zeta Tau Alpha sorority in the 1980s.

Was there a cafeteria on campus in the 1800s?

Students were required to eat at the campus dining hall, named Steward's Hall, and were banned from eating off campus until after the Civil War.

Where was Steward's Hall located?

This original Steward's Hall was located where Harper College is today. It was demolished in 1848 to make way for the construction of Harper, and the name Steward's Hall was transferred to a building near the corner Greene and Main Streets, where the School of Education is located today. The third and final Steward's Hall was constructed at the corner of Sumter and Greene Streets in the early 1900s. It was the main cafeteria for many years, but students were no longer required to eat on campus. It was demolished in 1950 to make way for the construction of Sumwalt College.

What were the Carovets Apartments?

After the end of World War II, a huge influx of veterans enrolled in the university under the GI Bill. The campus didn't have facilities for married veterans and their families, so the institution acquired surplus military housing units. The Carovet Apartments (Carolina + Veterans) were located on Bull Street near the State Hospital. They included a playground, clubhouse, and childcare services. The buildings were gradually torn down from the late 1950s into the early 1960s.

Did the university ever provide any other housing for married students?

University Terrace apartments served as on-campus housing for married students until its demolition in 1995 to make way for the Bull Street parking garage. The university didn't build the apartments, but purchased them from the city in the 1950s.

What was the first major building constructed after World War II?

Petigru College, built in 1950 as the new law school, was the first major construction project on campus since 1943. It was named for James Petigru, a noted South Carolina attorney and former US district attorney.

What was controversial about the design of the Russell House?

The building's modern brick design set a new standard for architectural style on campus and was harshly criticized for being too much of a drastic and unattractive change from the campus's traditional architectural styles. It is named for President Donald S. Russell and his wife, Virginia Utsey Russell, both of whom are alumni of the university.

When did the university first provide fraternity housing?

McBryde Quadrangle, also known as Fraternity Row, was constructed in 1955 as fraternity housing. Sorority housing was located in South Tower.

What residence halls were criticized for resembling air conditioning units?

The Towers, also known as the Honeycombs.

What design feature led to that nickname?

The nickname "Honeycombs" is a reference to the veil blocks pattern that covered the exteriors of the buildings. They were built in sets of two in 1958, 1962, and 1965. Demolition of the buildings began in 1996 to make way for the Graduate Science Research Center and the Honors College residence hall.

Name the buildings that used to be elementary schools.

McMaster College was constructed in 1911 as a public grammar school. It was named for Colonel F. W. McMaster. The university acquired the property in 1960 and renovated it for the School of Music. It now houses the School of Visual Art and Design.

The Benson School was originally the Wheeler Hill Elementary School for Negroes. It was later named for longtime teacher Florence C. Benson. The university acquired the building after the school closed in 1976. It now houses university offices.

What was the last building constructed inside the old Horseshoe wall?

The original Coker College building was constructed in 1962, inside the corner of the wall at Sumter and Greene Streets. It was originally the home of the College of Pharmacy and the Department of Biology. It was named after David R. Coker, an acclaimed agricultural statesman, alumnus, and former trustee.

Why is it no longer named Coker?

When pharmacy and biology moved into the newer Biological Sciences Center in 1976, the old building was renamed the Health Sciences Building and the Coker name transferred to the new building. The Health Sciences Building was renovated for the School of Journalism in 2015 but has not been named.

When did residence halls get so large?

Residence halls (and other campus buildings) jumped in size beginning in the 1960s. Student enrollment shot up, and the university moved into an era of mid-century modern architecture with tall buildings of concrete and steel. Patterson Hall (1962) and South Tower (1965) were the first residence halls over three stories tall.

Is there really a rotating restaurant on campus?

The Top of Carolina is a rotating dining facility on top of Capstone House. Capstone, Carolina's first honors residence hall, was built in 1967. The South Carolina manufacturer Robert G. Wilson acquired the rotating platform and mechanism from an exhibit at the New York World's Fair and gave it to the university.

Why is it on top of a residence hall?

Why not?

Is Capstone really named for a Confederate naval officer?

No, the building was named Capstone because it was the crowning point of the East Campus. The campus folklore about the name developed after a tongue-in-cheek editorial claimed it was named for Commodore Epaminondas J. Capstone, a Carolina graduate and Civil War hero. A postcard manufacturer didn't realize it was a fictitious story and printed it on a picture postcard of Capstone.

What was notable about Bates House residence hall?

Bates House's construction in 1969 marked a significant change from Carolina's usual residence hall design. It was intended to move away from the standardized institutional approach in the layout of the rooms and, instead, provided personalized living quarters through a variety of room arrangements and colors.

What about Bates West?

Completed in 1974, Bates West was the university's first coed residence hall. Both buildings are named for alumnus Jeff B. Bates, who served as South Carolina State treasurer from 1940 until his death in 1966.

When was Greene Street closed to traffic in front of the Russell House?

As the student population grew in the 1960s, the rising amount of student foot traffic across Greene was in constant conflict with vehicular traffic. Students began actively pressing for the closure of that portion of the street in the 1970s. Eighteen students were arrested at a demonstration in 1975. Columbia City Council finally agreed in 1977 to close it during certain hours on weekdays. It is now permanently closed to traffic.

What academic structure is actually two separate buildings connected by a central lobby and elevator?

The Close-Hipp Building. The university constructed a new building for the School of Business in 1973; ten years later, an identical structure was constructed and connected to the first. The first building was named for H. William Close, an executive with Springs Industries. The second building was named for Francis M. Hipp, chairman of the Liberty Corporation and former president of the USC-Business Partnership Foundation.

How many law school buildings have there been?

Four. The first was Petigru College in 1918. When the second law building was constructed in 1950, the Petigru name was moved, and the old building was renamed Currell College. The Law Center at Main and College Streets was built in 1973 to replace Petigru. Renovations completed in 2020 have turned it into academic and laboratory space. The fourth law school building opened in 2017 at the corner of Bull and Gervais Streets.

What is the Commissioners Oak?

A historical marker was placed in front of the 1973 Law Center to commemorate the South Carolina Commissioners Oak. The commissioners who were appointed to lay out the city of Columbia were said to have met in 1786 under an oak that grew at the site.

What is the triangle-shaped building on the south campus?

Swearingen Engineering Center was built in 1987 to expand the School of Engineering facilities. It is named for alumnus John E. Swearingen, chairman of Standard Oil Company.

What error was discovered on the outside railing of the Music School?

The railing is designed with the opening notes of the alma mater. However, during installation several notes were attached upside down.

What items did students place in a 1977 time capsule on the Horseshoe?

The contents included a pair of blue jeans, a T-shirt, and a pair of topsiders; a football signed by the 1977 football team; computer punch cards; a copy of *Playboy* magazine; a pack of cigarettes; a Farrah Fawcett poster; an empty bag from McDonald's; a Wham-O Frisbee; and a copy of Daniel Hollis's history of the university. The 1977 capsule was unearthed in October 2001.

What did students place in the time capsule buried in front of McKissick in 2001, as part of the university's bicentennial celebration?

Bicentennial printed items, a Hootie and the Blowfish ticket from their Homecoming weekend concert, Gamecock teams' athletic jerseys, three books about Carolina that were published during the bicentennial, a newspaper story in *The Gamecock* about beating Clemson's football team that year, movies, music CDs, and sealed personal letters to be opened along with the time capsule in 2051.

What is the only twentieth-century building on the Horseshoe?

McKissick Museum. It was constructed as the university's new main library in 1940, behind the original President's House. It was named McKissick Library, following President J. Rion McKissick's sudden death in 1944.

McKissick Museum circa 1944. Courtesy of the University of South Carolina Archives.

When did it become a museum?

After the opening of a new undergraduate library in 1959, now Thomas Cooper Library, McKissick became the graduate library. After Cooper was expanded to become the main library in 1976, the university's museum collections were placed all together in McKissick. It was formally rededicated as McKissick Museum in 1984.

What is the first building USC named for a Black woman?

The Celia Dial Saxon residence hall, in 2023. Saxon was one of Columbia's most revered educators, who taught for fifty-seven years. She was a student at the State Normal School for Teachers that was hosted by the university during Reconstruction.

What is the clapping circle?

The clapping circle is a round pattern of cobblestones between the Russell House patio and Davis Green. A person who claps their hands while standing in the center of the circle only hears a faint squeak instead of a clap. The effect wasn't intentional, and it's unknown who first noticed the phenomena.

What unusual sculpture used to be in the wall next to the Russell House patio?

Student Danny Berry created a four-foot bronze sculpture to place in a hole in the brick wall around the Russell House patio. The 1980 piece titled *The Wall* features a hand reaching out from the hole to grasp the metal rail on the wall. Smaller hands and clenched fists are underneath it, and a face is set into the bricks. Berry installed it without the university's permission. It was removed some time in 1987 or 1988.

What strange item was discovered inside a wall in Legare College in the 1920s?

A gamecock skeleton.

What eerie discovery was made behind DeSaussure in 2009?

DeSaussure College housed the university's first medical school, which operated from 1867 to 1873. In 2009, facility workers uncovered skeletal remains in a cadaver pit behind the building's east wing. The skeletons' multiple cut marks indicated that they were used by the university's medical students during dissection courses.

What structure has small figures of swimmers on the outside?

The Longstreet Theatre annex has small figures below the roof line because it was originally a natatorium, or indoor swimming pool. It was added to the rear of the building as part of the extensive building program funded by the Works Progress Administration. It opened in 1939. After Longstreet was converted into a theater in the 1970s, the natatorium was converted into the theater's scene shop, costume workshop, and equipment storage area.

Why is there a smokestack near the horseshoe?

The brick smokestack is all that remains of the old coal-fired heating plant that once stood in the area. The plant was built in the 1930s and demolished some thirty years later. The smokestack was left as a campus landmark.

Why does the smokestack have "USC" on it in both brick letters and in paint?

When the smokestack was built, the letters USC in white brick were included at the top. During his administration in the 1980s, President James Holderman promoted the use of "The USC" as a nickname for Carolina. It was part of his efforts to raise the public and academic profile of the U university, and it was a challenge to the University of Southern California since the University of South Carolina was founded before California was even a state. The letters were painted on the top of the smokestack as part of that promotion. More recently, they were painted over entirely and replaced with the current USC.

What Grammy-winning group performed on the Horseshoe in 1996?

Hootie and the Blowfish performed a live, nationally televised concert on the Horseshoe. All of the band members attended the university.

What unfortunate damage happened on the Horseshoe due to the concert?

An equipment truck collapsed a seal on an underground well.

Why are there wells on the Horseshoe?

Between 1805 and 1900, South Carolina had several wells for drawing water for drinking, cooking, and cleaning. The wells were filled in during a yellow fever outbreak in the late nineteenth century to help prevent the spread of the illness.

Have they ever been excavated?

A major archeological survey on the Horseshoe grounds was conducted by the South Carolina Institute of Archaeology and Anthropology during the 1970s and included excavation of the wells. The team found numerous artifacts, including vessels for drinking alcohol, porcelain and ceramic bowls and plates, glass, nails, and a US Army uniform button.

Did the archeologists discover anything else?

They uncovered the original foundation of DeSaussure College, which is located just 220 feet north of Rutledge, or one hundred feet further south than the completed building. If the college had continued with the building's construction in its original location, the Horseshoe grounds would have been much narrower.

When was the Horseshoe driveway bricked over?

The driveway was bricked over during the 1970s Horseshoe renovation project. It was done as part of the changes made to make the Horseshoe a pedestrian-friendly park-like space. The Horseshoe was also closed to vehicles at that time.

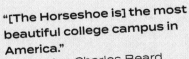

"[The Horseshoe is] the most beautiful college campus in America."
—Historian Charles Beard

Where did the university get all those old bricks?

The university has stockpiled old bricks for many years to have them available for repairs and other projects. Many of the driveway bricks, however, proved to be controversial, because they were from Booker T. Washington, the first Black high school in Columbia, South Carolina. After the school system was desegregated, the university acquired the property in 1974. The oldest building in the complex was deemed too expensive to renovate, so the university tore it down and used the bricks to pave the Horseshoe drive. Alumni of the high school were furious that USC students were walking over their beloved school.

Where was the original entrance to the campus located?

The center of the Sumter Street side of the Horseshoe wall. This gave the dirt road on the campus an oval shape, resembling a racetrack.

Are the mounds on Gibbes Green burial grounds?

No. The Gibbes Green area was originally very flat. The mounds were added during utilities work in the 1960s simply as a landscaping point of interest.

Are there tunnels that run under the campus and all the way to the river?

No. There are some utility tunnels on different sections of campus that contain high voltage lines, but the story of a network of tunnels or catacombs is just a myth.

What dormitory was the primary residence of African American students during Reconstruction?

The majority of students from 1873 to 1877 lived in Legare College.

What infrastructure used to be called "Brunton's Folly?"

As the east campus expanded in the 1960s and 1970s, more students were crossing the very busy Pickens Street. They campaigned to have the city close the street to traffic, but Vice President of Operations Hal Brunton pressed for a different option—a pedestrian bridge over Pickens Street, connecting the central and east campuses. The students were unhappy with the project and named it "Brunton's Folly." The bridge project required the City of Columbia to lower the section of Pickens Street between Bull and Greene Streets so trucks could fit under the bridge.

What rumor surrounded the construction of the Pickens Street bridge?

It was rumored to have been built to help the National Guard get troops and tanks between the central and east campuses in case of a student riot.

What originally stood in the courtyard between the humanities buildings and Gambrell?

The courtyard originally included a reflecting pool with an aquamobile titled *Drinking Birds*. Designed by Lynn Emory, the sculpture was commissioned by the university and installed in 1972. It had moving parts set in motion by running water.

Why was it removed?

It had problems staying in motion, and in a few years the birds had stopped moving entirely. The sculpture was removed, and the pool was replaced by a brick patio in the 1990s. A restaurant was built on the site in 2006.

How did ducks end up living in the Thomas Cooper Library reflecting pool?

Ducklings were abandoned in the pool after Easter in 1976. They survived and multiplied, and the reflecting pool was also referred to as the "duck pond." Although the ducks were a popular attraction, they sometimes suffered from attacks by animals and humans. The flock was moved to the pond in the A. C. Moore Garden in 1987. In the last several years, however, the reflecting pool has become a wildlife nursery again—this time for frogs.

What were the vulture lots?

The green spaces on either side of the Thomas Cooper Library reflecting pool used to be metered parking lots. Students, especially those who lived off campus, would circle and circle the lots like vultures, waiting for a space to open up so they could go to the library. The lots were converted to green spaces in 2000.

How many trees are on the Columbia campus?

Just over ten thousand.

Was there a golf course on the Columbia campus?

Gibbes Green, behind McKissick Museum, hosted a small course in the early 1900s.

Who is buried under the Maxcy Monument?

No one!

What is the Maxcy Monument?

It is a memorial to the first president of South Carolina College, Jonathan Maxcy. It was commissioned by the Clariosophic Society, one of the two antebellum student organizations. Noted South Carolina architect Robert Mills designed the monument. The monument was placed in the center of the Horseshoe and completed in 1827.

What is it made of?

The monument has a granite base, a white marble obelisk, and a marble cap ornamented with honeysuckles and symbols of immortality. The top of the obelisk has a bronze tripod that holds a bronze sphere. The granite base has insets of white marble tablets inscribed with epitaphs in Latin. The sphere was not originally attached to the cradle, but after numerous pranks in which it was stolen, the university welded the two pieces together.

Why were the inscriptions in Latin?

At the time, the students were required to study Latin, so they were all able to read them. Bronze markers with the English translation have since been placed at the base of the monument.

When was Thomas Cooper Library built?

The original section was constructed as the undergraduate library in 1959. It was designed by Edward Durell Stone and Lyles, Bissett, Carlisle, and Wolff and won the First Honor Award from the American Institute of Architects in 1963. The large, partially underground addition was completed in 1976. It is named after South Carolina College's second president, Thomas Cooper.

Why did it need such a large addition?

The rapid jump in student enrollment in the 1960s and 1970s quickly outgrew the library facilities. The addition transformed the building into the main campus library.

Is the bottom floor of Cooper Library the lowest point in South Carolina?

No, not even close! It isn't even the lowest point on campus, or in Columbia, since the land the campus is on slopes downward toward the river. However, it is the only building that has five underground levels.

What nickname have students given to the library?

TCoop.

Were the gold metal curtains in Thomas Cooper Library installed because of birds hitting the windows?

No. The curtains are part of the building's original design and are merely decorative.

Are those headstones in front of the War Memorial building?

The granite stones with bronze markers are memorials to the twenty-eight alumni who died during World War I and the Mexican border conflict. The markers were placed at the base of memorial elm trees in 1927. Over time, the trees died, and the landscape on that corner changed significantly. The markers were damaged, buried, and lost. Only half were able to be located and installed at the War Memorial grounds in 2018. The missing ones are being reproduced.

When did the library collections surpass one million volumes?

Cooper surpassed one million volumes in 1971–72.

When was Bull Street closed on campus?

In 1927, the City of Columbia finally agreed to close the section of Bull Street between Pendleton and Greene Streets after years of traffic issues that cropped up with the university's expansion.

When did the university start providing furnishings in the dormitory rooms for students?

The year 1926 was the first time that students did not have to purchase their own furniture for the dormitories.

Where was the first campus lounge for women students?

In 1912, women were provided a converted coal room in the old President's House to use as a lounge.

Where was the first infirmary on campus?

In 1888, the institution built a wooden house on College Street as the first permanent infirmary, in response to an outbreak of measles in 1886. Prior to this, there was only one makeshift room in Steward's Hall hat served as an Infirmary. The 1888 house was an improvement but still not an appropriate location for the infirmary.

When was the Thomson Infirmary built?

In 1907, Anne Jeter donated $15,000 to the university to build a new infirmary in honor of her late nephew, alumnus Wallace Thompson. The infirmary was completed in 1908 at the corner of Bull and Green Streets. It was the first time the university had a facility adequate to care for the health of students. The current Thompson Student Health Center was built in 1973. The name was moved along with the building.

When was the first telephone installed on the campus?

Telephones were installed in Columbia in 1880, but the first one did not arrive on campus until 1884. It was placed in the president's office.

When did electricity get installed on the campus?

Dormitories and professors' houses were wired for electricity in 1902.

When was modern plumbing added to the campus?

Modern plumbing was difficult to install on the campus. In 1898, in order to bathe, students had to either carry water to their rooms or go to one of the six showers in the basement of the science hall (Longstreet Theater). In 1902, President Woodward and the board of trustees requested money from the state legislature for a sewer system. In 1909, students still had to go to the gym for baths and showers, and they were still using outhouses. Additionally, no buildings had central heat, although other state colleges had already installed it in their buildings. Dormitories were still heated by fireplaces and students had to buy their own wood and coal. The last of the old buildings received central heat in 1926.

What popular activity in the 1890s damaged the Maxcy Monument?

Bonfires near the Maxcy Monument became a popular activity in the 1890s, but in 1895 a fire too near the monument blackened the stone and cracked one of the marble inset tablets.

When were intramural games first played?

Intramural games were approved by the faculty in 1890.

Where was the first athletic field on campus?

The first athletic or playing field was the eight acres of land formerly used for the farm bounded by Sumter, Devine, Bull, and Green Streets, where the Russell House and Thomas Cooper Library are located now. It was set up in 1890.

Why was the college library only open during daylight hours?

Due to concerns over fire, no candles or lamps were allowed, so the library was only open during daylight hours.

When were campus buildings first named for people?

The trustees named the buildings after prominent alumni and South Carolinians beginning in 1848. Rutledge and DeSaussure were originally South and North buildings, then Old South and Old North after new buildings were constructed. When two more buildings were constructed in 1848, the trustees decided to name all of the buildings.

What is the modern building next to the garden of Lieber College?

The freestanding broadcast studio was constructed in 2015, adjacent to the journalism building. Construction of the "greenhouse studio" was funded by an anonymous $1.5 million gift.

What is the name of the Lieber College garden?

The Columbia City Garden Club memorial rose garden is on the east and west sides of Lieber College. It was originally developed by the club in 1960 to honor deceased club members and was placed behind the South Caroliniana Library. It was moved in 1978 to Lieber. The three-tiered fountain was dedicated to Carolina first lady Norma Cannon Palms in appreciation of her interest in maintaining the memorial rose garden.

What special recognition did the university receive for its arboreal stewardship?

It earned a tree campus USA designation from the Arbor Day Foundation, and the Horseshoe trees have been named heritage trees of South Carolina.

What is the garden next to the Osborne Administration Building?

The Desegregation Commemorative Garden honors the three African American students who enrolled in the university in 1963. Garden features include a trinity of sculpted juniper topiaries, brick pathways, flower beds, and a granite monument etched with an original poem written by university poet Nikki Finney. The bricks in the pathways transition from solid to multiple colors to represent the university's desegregation.

Where is Anne's Garden?

Anne's Garden is behind the Public Health Research Center and features a bronze fountain called *Las Palomas* designed by wildlife sculptor Sandy Scott.

It is named for Carolina alumna and Columbia Green founder Anne Rainey. The Spanish name translates into "The Doves."

Where is the A. C. Moore Garden?

The garden is in a secluded spot on the corner of Blossom and Pickens Streets. It features a small duck pond, flowering shrubs, and shady trees. It is named for botany professor Andrew Charles Moore, who twice served as acting president of the university.

Where are some additional sculptures on campus?

The *Eternal Flame* is an eighteen-foot stainless steel installation created and donated by Leonardo Nierman, and is on display in the Palmetto Courtyard at the Darla Moore School of Business.

The *Longstreet Patio Fountain* was created by Carolina alumnus and sculptor Alan J. Sindler. The concrete sculpture was an interpretation based on a design concept by Robert LaForce and was installed on the patio behind Longstreet in 1975. Sindler reinterpreted the fountain in stainless steel in 2008.

The *AIDS Awareness* sculpture at the Koger Center is of a woman holding an AIDS quilt. It was created by Lexington artist Estelle Frierson and is symbolic of the university's commitment to community outreach, education programs, and research concerning HIV and AIDS.

Where are the two sculptures by Anna Hyatt Huntingdon?

The *Torchbearer* is in front of the College of Education. The heroic statue represents the passing of knowledge from generation to generation. *Fillies Playing* was installed in the McMaster College courtyard in 1960. Vandals sawed through the two aluminum horses from their base in 1965. One filly was recovered and put back on display, but it was nearly destroyed during renovations to McMaster in 1998 when it was accidentally tossed in a construction landfill. The sculpture was recovered after a faculty member intervened; it was restored and rededicated in April 2002. The second filly remained lost until July 2003, when workers clearing a residential property in Richland County discovered the sculpture, and it was returned to the university. They are on display inside McMaster College.

Where are the two sculptures of Carolina's mascot?

The *Cocky* statue sculpted by Robert Allison is seated on bench near Melton Observatory and Davis College. The *Gamecock*, a mammoth bronze piece sculpted by Jon Hair, anchors Springs Brooks Plaza at Williams-Brice Stadium. It's made of more than one hundred individual bronze castings welded together.

ATHLETICS

What was the first organized sport on campus?
Fencing. In 1836, the trustees hired a fencing instructor.

What was the first collegiate sport at the University of South Carolina?
Baseball arrived first in the 1880s. Intramural college teams played each other and against teams of city police, firemen, and mechanics. Intercollegiate contests began in the early 1890s, but Carolina did not officially permit such competitions until 1895.

When and where was the first intercollegiate Carolina football game?
On December 24, 1892, in Charleston, South Carolina. They played against a more experienced Furman College team and lost 44-0.

Was this a sanctioned game?
No. The faculty had prohibited intercollegiate sports, so the students had to sneak away to Charleston. Carolina's team had no coach, no experience, no uniforms, no team name, and no chance of winning. The team was formed so hastily that it included two non-student members. Team member Singleton Green played under an assumed name because his father was so opposed to football.

What was Carolina's first official football game?

The first game sanctioned by the trustees was on November 3, 1894, against the University of Georgia. The game was played at the state fairgrounds racetrack in Columbia. Carolina lost 40-0.

When was the first intercollegiate baseball game?

Carolina played Wofford on May 2, 1895, in Columbia. The Gamecocks lost 7-4.

Why was football banned at Carolina in 1906?

Nationwide, the sport's violence had raised many concerns, including at the national government. Players were receiving severe injuries in the game and there were some deaths as well. US president Theodore Roosevelt even considered banning football nationwide.

1896 Carolina baseball team. Courtesy of the University of South Carolina Archives.

When did it come back to campus?

The ban only lasted for one year. In 1907, the board of trustees allowed intercollegiate football to be played again after being bombarded with petitions from Carolina students and alumni.

What was the average weight of a football player in the early 1900s?

150 pounds.

When did Williams–Brice Stadium switch to artificial turf?

Artificial turf was installed for the 1971 season, prompting from fans and former players that the field had essentially been "paved." Natural turf returned for the 1984 season.

What bumper sticker was created in response to the disposal of artificial turf?

"Cocks kick ass on natural grass."

How was that bumper sticker revised after Pope John Paul II held a worship service at Williams–Brice Stadium in 1987?

"Cocks kick ass on *holy* grass."

What is the Palmetto Bowl?

The official name of the Carolina–Clemson game, decided on by both teams in 2014.

What record did the Carolina–Clemson rivalry hold until 2020?

The Carolina–Clemson football game held the distinction of being the longest-standing streak of play in a non-conference rivalry in the country. The Gamecocks and Tigers played each another for 111 straight seasons until 2020, when they were forced to take off a year from non-conference play due to the COVID-19 pandemic.

When did women's athletics start?

Women students founded their own sports teams just a few years after women were admitted to the university, but the teams were intramural clubs until the 1960s/1970s.

What were women's first intramural sports?

Lawn tennis, gymnastics/tumbling, rhythmic dance, and basketball. Their "uniforms" were just long skirts for tennis and bloomers for basketball (loose-fitting trousers, gathered at the knee or the ankle).

Who is the longest-serving football coach in Carolina history?

Rex Enright served as head football coach from 1938 to 1956. He also served as athletic director from 1938 until his death in 1960.

Who is the winningest football coach?

Steve Spurrier.

What was Big Thursday?

Big Thursday was name given to the annual Carolina–Clemson football game, because it was always played on the Thursday of State Fair Week, in Columbia.

When was the first Big Thursday game?

November 1, 1896.

When was the final Big Thursday game?

October 22, 1959.

Why did Big Thursday end?

Clemson coach Frank Howard had tried to change the game's arrangement for years, since it essentially gave Carolina the home field every year and did not allow the Clemson area to receive the economic benefits of all those sports fans. The change also put the rivalry game at the end of the season, giving it more build up than it had by being tied to the State Fair in the middle of the season. The end of the tradition upset many Carolina and Clemson fans.

Which coach built the basketball team into a national power in the 1960s?

Carolina fans were ecstatic with the hiring of basketball coach Frank McGuire in 1964. By 1968, he had crafted the Gamecock basketball team into a national power, filling the Carolina Coliseum with fans and regularly participating in post-season tournaments. They remained national championship contenders into the 1970s. McGuire later clashed with USC president James Holderman over the administration of the athletics department and left USC in 1980.

What was BAM?

The Buck-a-Month Club was a booster club for athletics established in 1939, and the forerunner of the current Gamecock Club.

Who was the first full-time baseball coach?

Former New York Yankee all-star Bobby Richardson became Carolina's first full-time baseball coach in 1969. Previous part-time coaches were usually an assistant football coach or physical education professor, although for the 1964–65 season it was English professor Bob Reising. Richardson quickly ramped up the program. The 1974 and 1975 teams broke multiple school records.

When did the Gamecocks first go to the College World Series?

The Gamecocks made their first ever trip to the College World Series in 1975 and advanced to the title game against Texas, losing 5–1. They returned in 1977 under new coach June Raines and again made it to the title game, losing to Arizona State University.

When did the baseball team win back-to-back national championships?

The Gamecocks won the College World Series in 2010 and 2011. They were the runner-up in 2012.

How many times have they been to the College World Series?

Eleven: 1975 (national runner-up), 1977 (national runner-up), 1981, 1982, 1985, 2002 (national runner-up), 2003, 2004, 2010, and 2011 (national champions), and 2012 (national runner-up).

How many Gamecocks have competed in the Olympics?

More than fifty.

When were women's sports moved from intramurals to the Athletic Department?

Until the passage of Title IX in 1972, women's sports at Carolina were at the intramural or club level. They did not have new equipment, team trainers, or doctors, and they had to rely on fundraisers to afford to participate in post season tournaments. Title IX forced the university to fund women's athletics at a level that would ensure them the same kind of quality equipment, uniforms, training, and coaching as the men's teams, moving them into the Department of Athletics.

What coach was known as "the man in black"?

Football coach Joe Morrison gained the nickname "the man in black" due to his all-black attire. He inadvertently started a fashion trend because Gamecock fans copied him by wearing all black to the games.

What was the "Black Magic" season?

Coach Joe Morrison came to Carolina in 1983. One year later, his football team achieved what came to be known as the "Black Magic" season. The team finished the regular season 10-1 with a close victory over Clemson and a number eleven rank.

What is arguably the most heartbreaking football game in Carolina history?

The 1984 Navy game shattered Gamecock hearts. Heading into that game, the team was undefeated and on its way to its first number one ranking in program history. Then Navy won.

What was the Fire Ant defense?

It was a nickname for football team defense in the 1980s and is especially associated with all-garnet uniforms and the 1984 Black Magic season. It refers to the way fire ants swarm around a threat, and the Gamecock defensive players would swarm around the ball at the end of a play.

In what conferences has Carolina been a member?

Southern Conference 1922–1953
Atlantic Coast Conference 1953–1971 (founding member)
Metro Conference 1983–1991 (except football and men's soccer, which were not sponsored by the conference)
Southeastern Conference 1991–

Why did Carolina leave the ACC?

Coach Paul Dietzel opposed the ACC's (Atlantic Coast Conference's) requirement of an eight hundred minimum SAT score to qualify for scholarships, which was higher than the NCAA (National Collegiate Athletic Association) standard. South Carolina coaches and trustees feared the ACC standard would divert talented athletes away from South Carolina to non-ACC schools. Ultimately, the board of trustees voted to withdraw membership from the conference and compete as an independent.

Which Gamecock sports are not sponsored by the SEC?

Men's soccer, which competes in the Sunbelt Conference, and women's beach volleyball, which competes in the Coastal Collegiates Sports Association.

Who won Carolina's first NCAA national championship?

The women's track and field team brought home the university's first-ever national championship in 2002.

What was football team's first bowl appearance?

The first Gator Bowl, January 1, 1946, in Jacksonville, Florida. Carolina lost to West Virginia 14–26.

When was the football team's first bowl game victory?
The Gamecocks beat West Virginia 24–21 in the 1995 Carquest Bowl.

When did the Gamecocks win back-to-back bowl victories?
Carolina defeated Ohio State in back-to-back victories in the 2001 and 2002 Outback Bowls.

When did the women's basketball team play in the Carolina Coliseum for the first time?
February 4, 1974—the first season they were a varsity team.

When was the first time the women's teams competed in NCAA tournaments?
In 1982, basketball, softball, swimming, and diving, and tennis all made NCAA post-season play.

When was equestrian added as a varsity sport?
In 1996, with Janet Brown as the inaugural head coach.

What was the original name of Williams-Brice Stadium?
Municipal Stadium. It was built by the city of Columbia in 1934. In 1935, the city transferred the title to the university and the school took over the remaining debt, and facility was renamed Carolina Stadium.

Carolina Stadium, now Williams-Brice Stadium circa 1935. Courtesy of the University of South Carolina Archives.

When did it become Williams-Brice?

The stadium has undergone multiple renovations and expansions since 1935, including the addition of the upper decks in 1972 and 1982. The renovations in the 1970s were funded in part by a gift from the estate of Martha Williams Brice of Sumter. The stadium was dedicated as Williams-Brice Stadium in 1972 as a memorial to Mrs. Brice, her husband, Thomas H. Brice, and her parents, Mr. and Mrs. O. L. Williams.

What is the stadium's nickname?

There are two: "Willy B" and "the Brice."

Why do Gamecock fans say, "If it ain't swayin', we ain't playin'"?

During the 1983 season, fans noticed the east upper deck would sway when the crowd was celebrating. Some reported it was moving by as much as one foot. It was especially noticeable during Carolina's route of Southern Cal 38–14. Coach Joe Morrison reportedly commented, "If it ain't swayin', we ain't playin.'" Giant shock absorbers were installed, and the deck was confirmed to be structurally sound. The phrase is still popular with fans, and the upper deck still sways a bit when the fans jump up and down.

What are the Cockabooses?

Twenty-two renovated cabooses parked behind Williams-Brice Stadium. The stadium is in an industrial part of the city with abandoned railroad spurs nearby. In 1990, a developer bought the land rights to one near the stadium, placed the stripped-down cabooses on it, and then sold them for $45,000 each. Twenty of them sold within forty-eight hours. All of the Cockabooses have a small kitchen, a bathroom, and a deck on the roof, but each owner has renovated and decorated theirs to suit their own taste as a prime tailgating spot. They now sell for hundreds of thousands of dollars.

Bunker! Tee!
Bunker! Tee!
Golf-sis! Boom! Bah!
Caddie! Caddie! Rah! Rah! Rah!
—1909 golf team cheer

Name the Gamecock player whose celebration on the field outraged Clemson fans.

Steve Taneyhill was the brash, long-haired quarterback who led the Gamecocks to an upset victory over the Tigers in 1992. He hit imaginary home runs after the Gamecocks scored downtowns, and then, after a key second-half touchdown, Taneyhill knelt on the Tiger Paw at midfield and pretended to sign his name. Tiger fans were outraged.

What was notable about the football game against North Carolina State University on September 4, 1999?

It was Lou Holtz's first game as coach, and it was played as the remnants of Hurricane Dennis lashed stadium with strong winds and driving rain.

Where did the Gamecocks originally play football on campus?

Before 1934, football games were played on Melton Field, now the location of the Russell House. When the trustees gave approval for intercollegiate sports in the 1890s, the area was converted into a baseball field named for Professor R. Means Davis, and a football field named for William Davis Melton who served as president of the institution from 1922 until his death in 1926.

When did Carolina play its first Homecoming game?

The first football game played in connection with Homecoming was on October 15, 1927, against North Carolina. The Gamecocks won 14-6.

What scandal disrupted the 1946 Carolina–Clemson game?

The 1946 Carolina–Clemson game was sold out, as usual, but some enterprising counterfeiters printed thousands of bogus tickets. When the fake tickets were discovered, pandemonium erupted. Fans broke down the large wooden gate at the stadium to push inside. There were so many extra fans that they spilled onto the sidelines and the field itself, at times interfering with the action and blocking the view from the stands. It was so bad that US secretary of state James F. Byrnes left his box seat for to watch from the sidelines, at times getting down on his hands and knees to peer between the legs of the Carolina coaches and players.

What was the greatest prank in Carolina history?

The 1961 Carolina–Clemson game was the first one played in Columbia since the end of Big Thursday. The Clemson band began playing "Hold That Tiger," and fans cheered as their football team trotted out onto the field to begin warming up. Things got strange very quickly as the players began doing the bunny hop, fell over backward during line drills, and pretended to milk cows. "Frank Howard" walked around spitting tobacco juice. When the confused Clemson fans realized there were imposters on the field making fun of their beloved Tigers, they stormed the field like a D-Day invasion force. Fortunately, the law enforcement officers at the game prevented a riot. The fake Tigers were members of the Sigma Nu fraternity in orange uniforms borrowed from a high school. They had walked onto the field unchallenged to pull off the greatest prank in the history of the University of South Carolina.

How did a foul ball start a brawl between the baseball team and the state militia?

On May 28, 1897, the baseball team was playing a team of the independent fire company of Columbia when two companies of the state militia arrived for drill. They were two days late for drill, but the compromise was to allow them to use the half of the field that was not being used for the baseball game. However, when a line drive fell and hit an officer's horse, General John G. Watts ordered the troops to clear the baseball teams off the field. The students fought back; Professor R. Means Davis was slightly hurt, and student Duncan D. McColl received a serious head injury and had to postpone his final exams until October. The general was reprimanded by a military court for his severe lack of judgment and unwarranted assumptions of authority.

What was a tramp athlete?

In the early 1900s, tramp athletes, or ringers, were essentially players for hire who moved from school to school. It was easy to pass as a student at the time because of the lack of a rigid registration system or registrar.

Where did the Gamecocks play basketball before the construction of the Carolina Coliseum?

Basketball was played in Carolina's gymnasium (now Longstreet Theatre) from 1911 to 1927, and the original Field House from 1927 to 1968.

Where was the Field House?

The university constructed the Field House in 1927 on Sumter Street, across from what is now Longstreet Theatre. At the time, it seated 3,500 people and was considered one of the finest basketball arenas in the South. The building was also used for student assemblies, freshmen orientation, J. Rion McKissick's inauguration as USC president, and May Queen ceremonies.

When was it replaced?

The booming campus population and the popularity of Coach Frank McGuire's teams in the 1960s made it difficult to get into the basketball games. The old Field House had also some close calls with fires in the building. Therefore, the university constructed a new arena, the Carolina Coliseum, in 1968. The old Field House was destroyed by fire in April 1968, shortly after the season ended.

What was the rumor about Frank McGuire and the Field House?

It was no secret that Coach Frank McGuire badly wanted the coliseum finished in time for the opening game of the 1968–69 basketball season, but there were concerns that it wouldn't happen. When the old Field House burned down in April 1968, forcing the escalation of the coliseum's completion, the rumor sprang up that McGuire himself had lit the match.

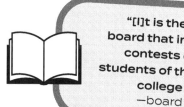

What was the nickname of the basketball arena?

The arena became known as "The House that Frank Built" due to the success and wild popularity of the Gamecock basketball team. In 1977, it was formally named Frank McGuire Arena. The Gamecocks moved into the Colonial Life Arena in 2002. The coliseum is being repurposed, and in 2015, the seats and the playing surface from McGuire arena were auctioned off.

What was the Roundhouse?

The Rex Enright Athletic Center was better known as the Roundhouse due to its unusual shape. It was constructed in 1956 to house the offices of the Department of Athletics and named for long-time coach and athletic director Rex Enright. The Roundhouse was demolished in 2013.

What was Sarge Frye Field?

The Carolina baseball field was named after Weldon B. "Sarge" Frye on May 11, 1980. Frye supervised the maintenance of the athletics facilities for forty-five years. The baseball stadium was demolished in 2010.

When did Carolina start playing "Sandstorm" at sporting events?

"Sandstorm" is an instrumental piece by Finnish DJ and record producer Darude. It was played during the South Carolina–Ole Miss game in 2009 and was an instant hit with the students. Since then, it has been incorporated into Gamecock sports venues.

What is the Carolina fight song?

The official university fight song is "The Fighting Gamecocks Lead the Way." Athletic director Paul Dietzel wrote the lyrics and set them to the tune "Step to the Rear." The song was introduced in 1968.

When did the football team start using the 2001 entrance?

Rated as the most exciting pregame entry in all of college football, "2001: A Space Odyssey" was first used in 1983. Over the years, the entrance of the team from the southwest tunnel in the stadium has added a gauntlet of smoke and the marching band, as well as Cocky's magical appearance.

Who was known as the Voice of the Gamecocks?

Bob Fulton was the voice of the Gamecocks for forty-three years, covering football, basketball, and baseball from 1952 to 1994. When he retired in 1995, his tenure with South Carolina was the fourth longest among NCAA broadcasters with one school. In 1990, he became the first non-coach or athlete to be inducted into the South Carolina Athletic Hall of Fame.

When was the Hall of Fame established?

The University of South Carolina Athletics Hall of Fame was established in 1967. Since that time, 197 individuals have been inducted, including former standout athletes, coaches, announcers, athletic trainers, and administrators associated with Gamecock athletics.

Who were the first inductees into the Hall of Fame?

Earl Clary, Sam Daniel, Freddie Tompkins, Alfred H. Von Kolnitz, and Steve Wadiak were all inducted in 1967.

Who was the first woman inducted into the Hall of Fame?

Sheila Foster in 1993.

Who is Carolina's Heisman Trophy winner?

George Rogers won South Carolina's first Heisman in 1980. He lead the nation in rushing and topped the hundred-yard mark in every game.

Who were the "First Eighteen?"

They were the first eighteen women to receive athletics scholarships at the University of South Carolina.

How many sports teams does Carolina have now?

As of 2024, there are eleven women's sports and nine men's sports teams.

> "The public has come to insist that the colleges furnish them with amusement during the autumn months. We can no more stem the tide than we can control the elements, but we are doing our utmost to exercise and maintain such control as not to allow it to interfere with the primary business of the University."
> —Melton, 1925

How many national championships does Carolina have?

Eight. There are five NCAA titles (women's outdoor track and field 2002; baseball 2010, 2011; women's basketball 2017 and 2022) and three national titles (equestrian 2005, 2007, and 2012).

What is the nickname for the soccer stadium?

Stone Stadium's location near a cemetery naturally gifted it with the nickname "the graveyard." The stadium opened in 1996 and was funded by a $1 million gift from the late alumnus Eugene E. Stone III.

When did the team leave Sarge Frye Field?

Founders Park, the Gamecock baseball stadium, opened in 2009 and is located on the banks of the Congaree River. The facility has the same field dimensions as Sarge Frye Field.

What is the Dodie?

The Dodie is the nickname for the Dodie Anderson Academic Enrichment Center built in 2010. It includes study lounges, computer labs, tutorial rooms, and dining spaces as well as Carolina's Athletic Hall of Fame. University alumna and Gamecock sports supporter Dodie Anderson provided a lead gift for the facility.

What is Gamecock Park?

The fifty-acre Gamecock Park provides a premium tailgating facility on the site of the former South Carolina farmers market near Williams-Brice Stadium. The 2012 site includes a central open space called the Garnet Way, a promenade that provides a route for the cheerleaders, marching band, and football team to walk through the venue on the way to the stadium.